A Mapmaker's

Dream

∽

Also by James Cowan

Poetry
African Journal
Petroglyphs

Nonfiction
The Mountain Men
The River People
Starlight's Trail
Sacred Places
Mysteries of the Dreaming
Myths of the Dreaming
The Aborigine Tradition
Letters from a Wild State
Messengers of the Gods
Wirrimanu
Two Men Dreaming

Translation
Where the Two Oceans Meet

For Children
Kunmangur: the Rainbow Serpent

A MAPMAKER'S DREAM

*The Meditations
of Fra Mauro,
Cartographer
to the
Court of Venice*

James Cowan

SHAMBHALA
Boston & London
1996

Shambhala Publications, Inc.
Horticultural Hall
300 Massachusetts Avenue
Boston, Massachusetts 02115

© 1996 by James Cowan

All rights reserved. No part of this book may be
reproduced in any form or by any means, electronic
or mechanical, including photocopying, recording, or by
any information storage and retrieval system, without
permission in writing from the publisher.

9   8   7   6   5   4   3

Printed in the United States of America

∞ This edition is printed on acid-free paper that meets
the American National Standards Institute Z39.48 Standard.

Distributed in the United States by Random House, Inc.,
and in Canada by Random House of Canada Ltd

Library of Congress Cataloging-in-Publication Data

Cowan, James, 1942–
    A mapmaker's dream: the meditations of Fra Mauro,
    cartographer to the court of Venice / James Cowan.—
    1st ed.
            p.   cm.
    ISBN 1-57062-196-9 (alk. paper)
    1. Mauro, fra, d. 1459—Fiction.   2. Cartography—
    Italy—Venice—History—Fiction.   3. Discoveries in
    geography—History—Fiction.   4. Venice (Italy)—
    History—697–1508—Fiction.   5. Cartographers—
    Italy—Venice—Fiction.   6. Monks—Italy—
    Venice—Fiction.   7. Fifteenth century—Fiction.
    I. Title.
    PR9619.3.C597M36   1996   96-7439
    823—dc20   CIP

I have often times and many ways looked into the state of earthly kingdomes, generally the whole world over (as farre as it may be yet knowen to Christian men commonly) being a studie of no great difficultie, but rather a purpose somewhat answerable to a perfect Cosmographer, to find himselfe Cosmolites, a citizen and member of the whole and onely one mysticall citie universall, and so consequently to meditate on the Cosmopoliticall government thereof, under the King almightie.

EDGAR, KING OF THE SAXONS.
CIRCA A.D. 973

I am my world.

LUDWIG WITTGENSTEIN

For
Arthur Versluis
cosmologoi

Contents

ະວເ

Introduction

I N THE LATE 1980S I made a visit to the island of San Lazzaro degli Armeni in the Venetian lagoon. At the time, I was research-ing the life of the poet Lord Byron, who had spent some months there while attempting to learn the Armenian language. He was in the habit of rowing over to the island from Venice three times a week in order to study in the monastery's voluminous library. Home of the Mechitar Fathers since 1715, San Lazzaro had been granted to the Armenian Church after the order was expelled from its monastery in Morea by the Turks. Since then San Laz-zaro has become a renowned center of learning, not only for Armenian exiles but for all those seeking after knowledge.

The Mechitar Fathers have always been regarded with

affection by visitors to Venice. It was only natural that their library, and the small museum attached to it, would become the beneficiary of numerous gifts from people as diverse as the duke of Madrid and even Napoleon. Pope Gregory XVI, for example, gave a marble bust of himself; and an eminent Armenian merchant from Egypt offered his collection of rare Oriental books, including some not altogether suitable copies of Sir Richard Burton's more salacious works.

The museum upstairs boasts an Egyptian mummy, a box full of manna, a collection of wooden carvings from Mount Athos, a Buddhist ritual scroll found by an Armenian traveler in a temple in Madras, and a small armory of antique weapons. There is also a machine for making electric sparks. More recent acquisitions include letters from Browning and Longfellow, a passage from the Koran in Coptic, and a set of German medals depicting the heads of British monarchs.

Superficial observation of such items led to my conjecture that the monastery had become the repository of a great deal of cultural bric-a-brac over the centuries. The Mechitar Fathers, like acquisitive bowerbirds, had collected and stored so many esoteric curios from the Levant that no researcher could possibly know where to begin. I had hoped to uncover a batch of Lord Byron's letters, or perhaps a notebook written in his hand. My disappointment in not doing so was partly allayed by the discovery of a copy of a journal written by a Venetian of the sixteenth century, a man named Fra Mauro who lived in the monastery of San Michele di Murano.

The discovery of Fra Mauro's journal had nothing to do with my own line of research. But it did not prevent me from dipping into its age-stained pages as a matter of idle curiosity. The title page aroused my interest at once. In the elaborate Italianate script of the day, Fra Mauro maintained that the thoughts inscribed therein were addressed only to himself. By chance I had discovered a rare confessional item containing the personal reflections of a late Renaissance cleric.

My attention diverted, I put aside my research into Lord Byron for a time and devoted my energies to a more detailed study of Fra Mauro. It was possible, after all, that such a journal might illuminate the mores of a time when Venice was at the height of its power and prestige. The personal statements of one man, however insignificant he might appear, could only serve to broaden our knowledge of this rich and fertile period. In the tradition of a Pepys, perhaps, Mauro's thoughts might have something important to say as a result of his personal encounters.

Imagine my surprise when I discovered that Mauro's observations were entirely undevotional. The man turned out to be a specialist in cartography, a mapmaker who devoted much of his life to drawing what he hoped might be a definitive map of the world. He was typical of many Renaissance scholars who regarded the study of the physical realm as being entirely worthy of their efforts. Leonardo da Vinci, and others like him, would have considered Mauro to be one of their own. The discovery of America by Columbus, and of the sea route around Africa to India by Vasco de Gama in the late fifteenth century merely emphasized the outward-looking demeanor of the age. For Mauro, the world had become his laboratory.

Little is known about Mauro's background. We do not know where or when he was born (though he intimates himself that he is a Venetian), nor in what year he died. There are no records of San Michele di Murano that we can turn to, since the monastery has long since been disbanded. How Mauro's journal came to be in the library of San Lazzaro is a mystery also. Probably it came to the Fathers by way of a gift from a Venetian benefactor. Nevertheless, what we do know is that Mauro was a consummate mapmaker. As most of the great cartographers of his day learned their trade in either Antwerp, Lisbon, or Genoa, one can only assume that Mauro had lived in the latter city at some stage in his life, possibly in his youth.

Underlying Mauro's desire to learn as much as he could about the physical world was a subtle expectation. Throughout his musings may be found evidence that he was seeking the existence of a more intrinsic reality, one that subsumed all others that the men of his time had known. Although he does not at any time articulate what the nature of this reality might be, Mauro clearly believed in its existence. Or shall I say that he *learned* to perceive the existence of this reality through the eyes of others, because this is the essence of his story.

Mauro represents an unusually creative example in the flowering of Renaissance thought. Here was a man who sought knowledge from the farthest corners of the world while remaining firmly ensconced in his own. He was content to allow others to do his observing for him. The merchants and adventurers who visited his cell, or wrote to him from afar, must have been seduced by his peculiar charm, for it appears that Mauro was extremely open to their experience and insights.

Still, one is amazed by his ability to accept such diverse information, and from so many sources, on its face value. Though his prejudices do sometimes manifest themselves (he is suspicious of Islam, for example), one gains the impression that he is more inclined to tolerance than its contrary. Nor does his personal belief as a practicing Christian monk become overbearing. One senses that he wears his Catholicity lightly, not wishing to allow church or doctrine to come between himself and the truth. In this sense he is typical of the worldliness of his age.

One feels that Mauro has something important to say, however—not just for his time but for always. The world that begins to unravel before his eyes is not so much a world of things as it is one of timeless forms. While he might be writing of one-eyed men, or the strange practices of headhunters in Borneo, one senses that he is more interested in trying to understand their motives, rather than merely recording their often despicable habits. He is not so much interested in what people do as in what they think. Mauro would prefer people to render their world in the form they hoped it might one day attain, rather than accept anything less.

This is not to say that Mauro was immune from the susceptibilities of his age. Though Europeans were already exploring the world with new eyes, more often than not they still believed in unicorns and one-legged men, rocs and fiery salamanders. On the one hand, we find Mauro recording material in his journal better suited to the pages of a medieval bestiary. On the other hand, we find him drawing conclusions from the reports he received that go far beyond the contemporary views of his time. In a rather strange way we see him stepping outside his time and viewing the world in its eternally repeated forms. To his way of thinking, the world undergoes change only in the human consciousness. As this consciousness changes, so too does the world.

Fra Mauro finds himself straddling two concepts of truth: the one unchanging, reinforced by medieval absolutism, the other conditional and largely determined by new and marvelous discoveries. For all his curiosity, we see him oscillating between the two. His informants provide him with all the ingredients required to lead an intense imaginary life, while at the same time he still clings to the comfort of certain dogmas and prejudices. We find his inwardness strangely appealing, however, because in it we see echoes of our own way of thinking. Throughout his journal we observe Mauro subjecting what he hears or reads to a most particular form of scrutiny. The man is unsure whether he exists in his own right, or whether he is merely the product of his own thought.

Something must be said about his informants. They range across the entire spectrum of sixteenth-century public life. Merchants, travelers, scholars, foreign legates, ambassadors, teachers, missionaries and officers—they all feed him information that he readily devours in the tranquil surroundings of his study. He is like a sponge, soaking up whatever his visitors have to offer. Mauro is not uncritical of their opinions, however, and we often find him analyzing their observations carefully. He is so captivated by the ability of these travelers to quit the familiar world, which he knew so well, that we sense he longed to break free from his restricted life as a cleric and join them on their journeys. We are left with the impression that Fra Mauro might have gladly traded places with these explorers and adventurers had he the courage to do so.

I decided that it would be an interesting exercise to translate Fra Mauro's journal. By doing so I hoped to throw some light on the whereabouts of the map he had been working on during his life, as it seemed strange that his journal should not be accompanied by what he speaks of so often. Either the map had become lost or it had been commandeered by Venetian authorities eager to preserve the preeminence of *La Serenissima,* that most Serene Republic, as a major seafaring nation.

No one can say categorically that his map does not exist. It may be that a more determined researcher than myself will one day discover it among the papers lying abandoned in the vaults of the Venetian archives. Perhaps his vision of the world lies mouldering in some drawer along with similar attempts by others. There may be many different maps of the world depicting its unfathomable surprise awaiting exhumation from the tomb of the past.

To those reading Fra Mauro for the first time, let me say this: always treat his ruminations as a process of gradual guessing. His dream is to derive meanings from the perfect use of mystery. Each place that he evokes becomes a symbol. Little by little he tries to evoke a country, an entire world, in order to reveal a frame of mind. In doing so he often chooses a piece of information, a mere fact sometimes, with the object of causing a new state of mind to emerge. He is trying to encourage a process of unlimited deciphering, as if these facts are but the tip of an iceberg. He is asking us to dispense with the ice floe of appearances and plunge ever deeper below its surface. It is up to the reader to determine whether Fra Mauro's meditations on the discovery of the world strike a sympathetic chord.

James Cowan
San Lazarro, Venice

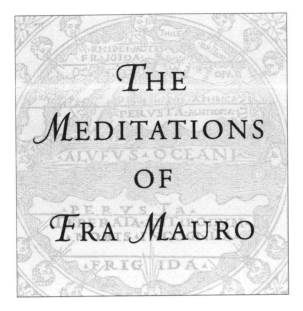

The Meditations of Fra Mauro

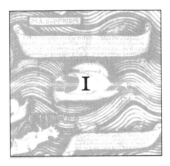

OR SOME TIME I have wanted to relate a circumstance that has been happening to me in recent years. I do not necessarily want my words to crackle like parchment or give off the aroma of old maps, but I do want them to reflect my deep interest in such things. I want to tell of a journey that I have been making, a journey beyond all known frontiers, that speaks of possibilities rather than anything so prosaic as what we already know.

There are precedents for such an undertaking. Christopher Columbus was looking for Paradise when he set out on his epic voyage across the Atlantic.* I have seen anno-

---

*Columbus was also deeply influenced by the Greek geographer Strabo, who corroborated Homer's views as to the sphericity of the

tations made by him to this effect in a treatise by Pierre d'Ailly of France, the *Tractatus de Imagine Mundi*—a view of an imaginary world. Both he and Columbus (who, I am told, carried d'Ailly's treatise with him on his voyage to the New World) were eager to represent accurately what was as yet undiscovered.

Nor were they the only men to think along such lines. Giovanni dei Marignolli, one of our ambassadors to China, was informed by the people of Serendip* that Adam's Peak, the glorious summit from which the world could be witnessed at a glance, was only forty miles from Paradise. They also informed him that on a fine day it was

ᴐᴂᴐᴂᴐᴂᴐᴂᴐᴂᴐᴂ

earth. Strabo believed the four points of the compass to have been situated somewhat differently than for us, for he says, "If the extent of the Atlantic Ocean were not an obstacle, we might easily pass from Iberia to India, still keeping in the same parallel." Columbus attempted to follow the parallel Strabo mentioned. Had he succeeded in doing so, he would have reached New York rather than the West Indies. Furthermore, assuming as he did that the American continent did not exist, then he would have sighted land to the north of Japan, somewhat north of the India of Strabo. Reinforcing the view that Columbus was likely looking for Paradise, we have a letter to Ferdinand Martins, a canon in Lisbon, by one Paul the physi-

cian, written in Latin from Florence, and dated 25 June 1474. The letter was later translated by Columbus's son, Fernando, when writing the life of his father. He had found it among his father's papers. In the letter the author tells of a city known as Quinsay: "The circumference of that city is one hundred miles. It possess ten bridges, and its name means 'The City of the Heavens.' The city is in the province of Mango, near that of Cathay. It will not be necessary, therefore, to cross very extensive spaces over the sea on an unknown route." Possibly Columbus took this advice to heart, and had decided to make his secret agenda the discovery of the city of Quinsay.

*A Medieval name for Ceylon, or present-day Sri Lanka.

possible to hear water cascading from a river flowing from Eden. He, like John of Hesse, who maintained that Purgatory lay in the Antipodes somewhere, wanted to locate certain places said to exist beyond the known world.

These men were keen observers of the imaginary. As a cartographer attached to the Order of Camaldules at San Michele di Murano here in Venice, I too have made it my life's task to chart the course of such men as they wander the byways of the earth. No seaman's tale is too trivial to hear, no traveler's journal too pedestrian to read. I have been at the mercy of other men's observations ever since I abandoned mathematics and physics in order to study the world that they had encountered.

For as long as I can remember I have wanted to travel. My name is Fra Mauro. I am a monk, mature in years and rather portly. To some I may even appear to be—well, let me admit it—somewhat lazy. My problem is that I have always been afraid of making such a journey, probably because my bones would renounce me as an imposter! It is as if the horizon that I witness at sea off the Lido and Sottomarina, whenever I make the occasional excursion to these places, were an unscalable wall, a barrier. Sometimes I have a strong desire to climb it, but I am still fearful of what might lie beyond. As a result I allow others to live for me, discovering peoples and realms of which I can only dream.

Cartography, however, is no idle pastime. Over the years I have learned to recognize the beauty of rhumb lines and wind roses. They are a navigator's delight, the lines along which every sailor voyages in pursuit of various points on the compass. Where these lines merge becomes their focus. They act as guides. At no time does a sailor reach beyond such a point whence he cannot return. Rhumb lines are the surest link he has with his past, indeed with himself. They keep him in contact with what he knows, with a familiar world.

Ptolemy* has always been my hero. Ever since I first read the eight volumes of his massive *Geographia* during my novitiate, I have been under his spell. He gave us the coordinates of latitude and longitude, the very principle of ordering the surface of the earth. How often have I burned a lamp far into the night poring over his maps, traveling into deepest Africa and across the mountains of the Parmir as far as India. Ptolemy introduced me to a mysterious world, a world at once held aloft in the hands of sages while being cooled by the breaths of cherub-faced winds.

So many names on maps invoke a sense of mystery.

---

* Ptolemy was a celebrated geographer and astrologer in the reign of Adrian and Antonius. A native of Alexandria, he received the epithets "most wise" and "most divine" among the Greeks. In his well-known system of the world, he placed the earth in the center of the universe. He accounted for the motion of heavenly bodies by way of an almost unintelligible application of cycles and epicycles, a doctrine universally believed and adopted by the learned until the sixteenth century, when it was refuted by Copernicus. One of his books gives a valuable account of the fixed stars, for 1,022 of which he gives the latitude and longitude.

India Orientalis, Maris Pacifici, Totius Africae, Pars Orbis, Americae—such a list of terrestrials! Every name conjures up a place peopled by turbaned Orientals, mermaids, and hooved men. I have gazed at many-armed figures and hairy-bodied women etched in the margins of these maps and asked myself why the world is as it is. So far I have not come up with any answers. The world continues to remain as enigmatic as the day I first attempted to make its diversity my own.

Of course, my asceticism has long been fueled by such considerations. But I have also been conscious that certain lines of inquiry can be dangerous. What lies beyond the margin of the world often sings to us with the voice of a siren, as if calling us into its embrace. We listen, we are lured, and finally we are seduced. The heavily scored margins on charts that I have observed over the years are testament to this predilection on the part of many seafarers. They are utterly bewitched by the prospect of continuing along one rhumb line until it reaches its farthest point. They want to find out whether its ultimate destination concurs with their idea of how the world really is.

Moreover, there is little difference between performing my rosary in chapel of a morning or fashioning a wind rose on a chart. Each is a form of meditation. A man staggers along the Via Dolorosa every time he sets out to create a thing of beauty. I have often thought that the fleur-de-lis on a compass card can be as difficult to render truthfully as the Lord's Prayer. Their very pointedness exacts its own kind of demand. They align themselves with all I know to be verifiable but cannot perceive with any degree of certainty myself.

I do not see my obsession with maps and travelers' tales as being in conflict with my spiritual concerns. Not in the least. My role as a cartographer is tantamount to the discovery of the world. Though sometimes spurned by my fellow friars as a thing of evil, I consider this world to be in no way different from that espoused by our Savior. It is yet another manifestation of His kingdom masquerading in the guise of multiplicity and change. As I see it, what tumbles forth from the lips of wayfarers can be as fragrant as myrrh emitted from a saint's bones on feast days.

Every compass I box in my mind directs me toward an imaginary land. I am seeking new ideas, visions. I do not wish to affirm what I already know. Each map I draw is made up of information I have received from visitors to my cell, as well as those ideas of my own that have been inspired by their sage and often noble and fantastical remarks. Strangely, though, I find myself living in the presence of what for them is already a retrospective moment. By speaking to me they are able to regain all that they might have thought forever lost.

It is a salutary event for us both: two men wrangling over an observation one man has perceived above all others. He is the master, I the slave. We sit on stools opposite one another, a breeze from the Adriatic cooling our faces on hot summer days. We gaze at maps that our eyes chart in each other's hearts. Together cartographer and adventurer argue over distances and routes while silently acknowledging that these are really only diversions, since we are struggling to make sense of disparate knowledge. We are like oar and rowlock, trying to exact a measure of leverage from one another, even as we acknowledge that we are probably traveling toward the same destination.

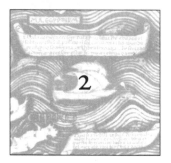

2

APITAL OF THE WORLD! yes, earth's navel, Jerusalem. The good Dante regarded it as all men's haven after that of his beloved Florence. Our Savior rendered up His corporeal existence there, within sight of its troubled walls. In my thoughts I have often tramped its alleys, suffered along with Him as He attempted to absolve me of my sins. Dung of all monks! Never in my life have I known what it is like to experience the full pain of knowing the truth.

It is my quandary, of course. Sometimes I think that every gateway leading into this city is barred by hard blocks of stone. Part of me longs to prostrate myself in the holy places and kiss the relics, while another part yearns to climb to the high, free spaces of the earth's summits. I am drawn toward action, but equally I withdraw from it. In an age wedded to money, trade, and the colonization of unknown places, I feel I am unable to contribute. I stand back and observe my compatriots' endeavors without sharing in their triumphs.

Who knows? A pilgrimage to the Holy Land might signal the beginning of my participation in life. Abd al-Malik's gate* beckons! Through it I might enter into a place wherein my appetite will be stimulated at last. Is it life from which I retreat, or is it life that retreats from me? The very fact that I think of myself and life as being separate suggests a break in the thread that binds me. I am like the lizard that has abandoned its tail in order to survive. The creature's tail and my life have been left squirming on the path.

The pilgrim's guides to Jerusalem that I have been fortunate enough to read at various times in my life have filled me with a very real excitement. They suggest a journey into a changed state, as if the long road up from Jaffa under the eye of marauding Saracens is but a prelude to a new life. One of these, written by the worthy Saewulf,† spoke of Christian corpses lying half-eaten by the road-

---

*Abd al-Malik's gate, known as the Gate Beautiful, was one of a number allowing entry into the Dome of the Rock in Jerusalem. It was said that Saint Peter and Saint John healed a lame man near its precinct. Later known as the Golden Gate by the Greeks, it was associated with the triumphal entry of Christ into Jerusalem on Palm Sunday. This story may have been invented to account for why the gate was blocked by Caliph Abd al-Malik during his reign in the Umayyad period.

†Saewulf, probably a Briton,

side, surely a sign that this gantlet is designed to tax old prejudices such as the "meaning of life" or the "noble Christian ideal." The Saracens, it appears, have other ways of defining such things.

Probably one has to accept their idea of the veil if one is to understand their antipathy toward us. Calling us infidel is also an old Saracen trick. True meaning lies as if hidden behind a series of waxed seals on an edict, each bearing the stamp of authority. Breaking one open only inspires the need to break open another. As each meaning crumbles under the pressure of knowing, so too does the essential meaning still await revelation.

This is the principle of the veil well known to the Saracens.* Those unfortunate Christians who met their deaths

---

made a journey to the Holy Land in 1101–2. A manuscript detailing his travels was found in the library of Matthew Parker, archbishop of Canterbury during the sixteenth century.

* Probably Mauro is alluding to a Koranic exposition of the Seventy Thousand Veils, where it says, "Allah has Seventy Thousand Veils of Light and Darkness: were He to withdraw their curtain, then would the splendors of His aspect surely consume everyone who apprehended Him with their sight." According to al-Ghazali, a noted Arab philosopher, there are three categories of veils: pure darkness, mixed darkness and light, and pure light. People are veiled by one or another of these in accordance with their spiritual temperament. They are thus dominated in varying degrees by (a) the senses, (b) the imagination and discursive intelligence, or (c) pure light. To those who attain to the "veil of light" God's epiphany comes in one rush, so that all is apprehensible by the sight of the Sense or by the insight of Intelligence, and the "splendors of His countenance are utterly consumed." Al-Ghazali likened this progressive unveiling (enlightenment) to the "Stations of the Way of the Light."

on the road to Jerusalem could be forgiven for believing that quitting home in the first place had been a mistake. Unfortunately, they, like those wax seals, had been broken and discarded before they could experience the vision they so desperately sought.

Jerusalem represents its own peculiar ambivalence. All my training as a monk has led me to believe that this really is the capital of the world. Here a miracle occurred. Here a man died as a God. Yet in a very real sense the city has weighed heavily on the shoulders of Christians ever since. Though His death was meant to have released us from the sin of Adam, it seems we are entangled in it more than ever.

I speculate. Mapmakers are entitled to do so, since they readily acknowledge that they are rarely in possession of all the facts. They are always dealing with secondary accounts, the tag ends of impressions. Theirs is an uncertain science. What they do is imagine coastlines, bluffs, and estuaries in order to make up for what they do not know. How many times do they sketch in a cape or bay without knowing the continent to which it might be attached? They do not know these things because they are constantly dealing with other men's observations, no more than a glance shoreward from the rigging of a passing ship.

I try to put myself in their position sometimes. Gazing into the distance evokes a kind of frozen wonder, as if space were indeed unlimited. Who am I to be so convinced that all this emptiness is not the manifestation of

some invisible substance? Even the lazy flight of an alba-
tross cannot diminish the sheer presence of what is not
there in the first place. I ask myself sometimes whether my
eyes may be playing tricks. But no—an unbroken skyline
signals that my desire to see something special beyond it
remains forever unappeased. Like Jerusalem, I will just
have to live with it as the nearest thing to a celestial image
that I will ever know. Air, too, I must learn to accept for
the invisible substance that it is.

Such ruminations tell me one thing about myself: that
my penchant for undiscovered coastlines populated by
savages reminds me of how far I have become removed
from the contours of my own city. Venice! This lagoon of
soupy canals, cats' pee, and pageants. Who might have
imagined that these islands could have imposed such a
stolid merchant mentality upon its people? Yet here we
are, warehouse to the Levant,* a principality of shopkeep-
ers awaiting the arrival of the next fleet from Constantinople or Cyprus. Through no fault of our own we have
learned to profit from trade, not ideas or the parrying of
concepts.

It does us no harm to be critical of ourselves. If nothing
else, we Venetians understand our limitations. We took
refuge on these islands in order to escape the barbarians
from the north. Were we not conscious of wanting to hold

---

*The Levant, a term denoting all
the countries of the eastern part of
the Mediterranean. The word is derived from the French word *lever,*
meaning "to rise" as the sun does
in the east.

on to something in the wake of their hunger for empire? This was not such a crime. Isolating ourselves among these marshes made us robust, pragmatic, given to opportunism, fine sailors, with a deep yearning to prove what we were made of. Everything we did or thought became an outward expression of ourselves. There was no room for the inward gaze, and contemplation we left to those peoples of the East who seemed so adept at focusing on the navel.* I say these things because I feel I should be honest. As a monk I have indentured myself to God. But as a man I have always been attracted by the sight of rolled rope on a deck, caravels newly caulked riding at anchor. I am torn between them—one a divine gift, the other a lure of the as yet unwitnessed. Each time a galley lowers its oars and

*Focusing on the navel was an early Christian practice devised by the hesychast monks of the Greek Orthodox faith. According to Saint John Climacus, a hesychast is one who strives to maintain that which is incorporeal (i.e., the mind) within the body. A technique of prayer integrated with breathing, the monks used to drop their heads in meditation, so gaining for themselves the derisive epithet of *omphalopsychoi* or "navel gazers" because it was believed by some that they situated man's soul in his navel. By reciting the Jesus Prayer continually and controlling his breathing, a monk might attain to a state of religious ecstasy. Saint Gregory Palamas, a noted Orthodox theologian, described the technique thus: "It is not beside the point, particularly in the case of beginners, to teach them to look into themselves and to direct their minds inward by means of breathing . . . until, with God's help, advancing to a greater perfection, [they] make their minds impermeable and impervious to all that surrounds them. They will be in a position to gather it together like a scroll neatly rolled up into one solid cylinder." He further maintained that *hesychia* (quiet) is "the standing still of the mind and of the world, forgetfulness of what is below, initiation into secret knowledge of what is above, the putting aside of thoughts for what is better than they."

sets sail from Rio Galeazzo to some foreign port, it carries with it my prayers for its safety. I pray for it because deep in my heart I want it to return with news of another world, where men are not exiled for committing some self-inflicted crime but live on islands of their own will, fashioning their own unique vision of what is right.

This much is true, though: I see the world as a series of clues that somehow explain the universe. Pachyderms and narwhals, talipot trees and insect-eating plants, flightless birds and boa contrictors—all are a part of some cryptic message that needs to be deciphered if we are to encounter its wholeness.

Nor are we the sole object of knowledge. Our thoughtfulness is integral to the observation of a porpoise frolicking at our bow, since it alone determines the level of joy we might feel. The sound of Saint Mark's bells pealing across the water at dusk is less the sound of clappers against brass, either; it is the echo of an invitation being extended to all of us to participate in something deeply imagined.

3

LL DESIRE I might have to quit this earth was originally provoked by watching a bird die from an arrow wound inflicted by me as a youth one day in the forest. The memory of its bleeding breast has left me scarred. Even now I see myself as that bird, once so freely able to fly, now brought down to earth. Sometimes I imagine the wound I inflicted as one the soldier inflicted on Our Lord at Calvary. Either way, I am aware of falling victim to an unholy desire to torture myself. It seems the bird in me has encountered mortality in such a wanton act, just as Our Lord must have done when the spear lanced His breast.

My daemons are hard at work this morning! In my gray stone cell smelling of candle wax I find it hard sometimes to shrug off what are, after all, only minor regrets. The inanimacy of a dead bird is a small event indeed when compared to the perturbations of my heart. My spirit is uneasy because I am constantly reaching out for something that defies all logic. Nor does my faith appear sufficient to encompass the great free space of my own yearnings.

That word again, compass! What but a lodestone can direct any of us toward that mysterious summer light said to exist in the Arctic? Men journey there, I'm told, on sleighs drawn by deer. They travel toward polar wastelands in pursuit of an invisible silence. To date no traveler has ever explained to me what it is that constitutes this silence. They have alluded to it, of course, and skirted its edges by way of intonation or gesture. They have helped me to feel its reality, its emptiness, its peculiar substance. But so far no one has been able to reveal it to me in any way other than that of his own sense of surprise.

When such travelers leave my cell after our meetings, I always assume that something has been left unsaid. The air is redolent with the echo of words whose articulation would have meant their defilement. We have parted, knowing that what we might have wished to say could not, in the end, be revealed. Why? All I know is that these men have accumulated in the frozen wastelands of the north impressions that preserve the contours of this silence. Surrounded by the soft padding of deer, they traverse a whiteness that is a silence, which is none other than their particular way of meditating.

Nonetheless, a collusion grows up between us, almost an intimacy. The silence they experience but can't explain is the silence I know whenever I go down on my knees to pray. My eyes take in the Cross, aware that throughout time we have tried to give expression to what lies beyond the purview of our hearts and minds. What we long for most eludes us. What we journey to the ends of the earth to find turns out to have departed a month, a day, even a minute before. We are left with the feeling that if we had only decided to act sooner rather than later, we might have discovered what we were looking for.

Take one intrepid traveler that I met recently. He came to me fresh from a long sea voyage, eager to share with me his knowledge. Salt was still in his beard. All his gestures were those of a man possessed by what can only be called the memory of a life-changing encounter. He told me of his journey to India, and how he had descended to the plain through the passes of the Pamir and Kush. A merchant by trade, he had gone there seeking spices and rare stones, but instead he had acquired something altogether different.

"I happened upon the tomb of Emperor Nizamuddin, in Delhi," he related to me one morning while we sat in the courtyard garden. Spring blossoms already stimulated our senses. "Built of red stones, it was surrounded by lawns littered with tiny flowers. Women, crouching on the grass, were cutting each blade as carefully as the hair on their own heads. Under the dome the emperor's catafalque lay like a small boat that had been beached. Pigeons flapped in the airy space above. After I had paid my respects to the memory of the emperor, I walked out through the main archway and looked up to see a cluster of green parrots gorging themselves on honey in the stonework. Imagine, parrots feeding on all this sweetness coming from an emperor's tomb!

"Only when I began to walk across the lawn did I realize the full significance of what I had observed. I was approached by the tomb's custodian, who asked me to watch where I placed my feet. He was afraid that I might have inadvertantly stepped on a bee as I walked. It seems he was anxious to ensure that these tiny creatures continued to survive, so that the tomb's spiritual power might go on unabated. In a rather strange way Nizamuddin's remains had become a focus for all this sweetness. Such qualities are considered to be very important to the worshipers of Brahma."

Imagine how I felt after my visitor had related to me his encounter with the bees of Nizamuddin. Here was a man who had witnessed what he believed to be a miracle. On one of the arches he had seen clusters of brightly colored parrots feasting on honey that had oozed from the stonework itself. The tomb's custodian had reinforced his belief by emphasizing the need not to tread on any stray bee for fear of disrupting the ideal conditions surrounding the emperor's last resting place. It was as if the tomb partook of a special quality of sanctity that set it apart from other edifices.

I realized at once that this was the form his silence had taken, and he had come to see me in the hope of sharing with me the very strangeness of his experience. To his disappointment, he had discovered that it was impossible to explain how he felt. It was only then that I began to understand why sojourners like he were constantly moving on in life, forever searching, hoping in the end to discover what others before them have failed to do.

The merchant had left me with a unique record of his experience. Miraculously, the incidents he had witnessed at Nizamuddin's tomb had been transported back over the mountain passes of the Pamir and Kush and, on his lips, had entered in triumph the lagoon of Venice. His story was more real to me now than all the spices unloaded from his ships.

How was I to inscribe what he told me onto my map? Was it possible to flaunt the bright plumage of those parrots as if it were the invisible substance of a wind rose? Or should I simply erase the words *Mare del Sud* from the ocean I had been working on and write *Mare d'Eluceo,* meaning "That Which Reveals Itself?" Without knowing it, my traveler from the East had revealed to me the cause of his silence; for he had journeyed to me across the polar wastelands of his own obsession with the inexplicable.

4

OMETIMES WHEN THE WIND is blowing in from the Adriatic I can hear the sound of mallet and saw drifting across the lagoon from the shipyards by the Arsenal. The raw skeletons of galleys are filled with men busily fleshing out hulls with wooden planks cut in the forests of Lombardy. This is the Venice that I have come to know and love. Campanile and portico, statue and arabesque, the smell of laurel leaf in a hidden garden—such are the impressions that make up this city. I become one of its gondoliers, dipping my pole deep into its murky waters.

Though I rarely stray forth from these monastery walls, all the world is at my fingertips. It journeys to me in the form of other men's impressions. As if in my throne room I await the visitation of my courtiers, their capes still stained with the dust of disappointment or delight. They come to me to unburden themselves. They look to me for advice. More than anything they want me to confirm the rightness of their endeavors. I am a beacon to them, glimmering on a rocky headland.

Am I overreaching myself? Why, of course! I have long since learned not to restrain my penchant for embroidering reality. A Celtic knot would be a bland thing were it not inspired by a vision, which is made concrete by the patience and care of a craftsman. Mapmakers embroider the world, and I am no exception. My maps are crafted to convey an illusion, this much is certain.

Every item of knowledge that comes my way is like a crust falling from a rich man's table. I reach for it hungrily. The famine in my heart drives me to savor its taste. Sometimes I even delude myself into believing I am a guest at the rich man's table. Why not? Hunger can drive a man beyond himself. It transforms him into one overweening appetite so that he finds himself in danger of becoming the crust.

I recall a scholar who visited me at a time when my eyes were still innocent to the ploys we use to escape death. He told me of an Egyptian mummy he had witnessed in the library of a friend. In minute detail the scholar described what he saw, so that to this day I can still see this mummy as if it were here in my cell.

It was a woman, the daughter of a priest. Her skin was black, though she possessed all her teeth. Her eye sockets were stuffed with tiny dollops of rotting shroud, and her nose lay partly collapsed against her face. Small, some might say petite, this young virgin priestess lay in her coffin, her head resting on a faded velvet pillow. Her slim arms and hands bespoke a delicacy, an almost ephemeral lightness of being, as if she had somehow managed to escape the consequences of her own mortality. According to my scholar friend the presence of this woman intimated a repose that he had never felt himself.

"In her death I encountered something rather strange," the scholar admitted to me, thoughtfully turning the pages of his notebook as he spoke. "It was as if her life had departed from her body in a flurry of wings, leaving her not a little surprised by its hasty departure. Yes, surprise, this describes her frozen expression well. She gave me to believe that even in death her life had provided her with something of a jolt. It is clear to me now that we do not engage in life so easily. It is not something we embrace naturally, as if it were ours by right. In a sense, we need to be jolted into it, do we not?"

The scholar went on to describe his own feelings after being in the library with the mummy. Though the mere idea of any transmigration of the soul was abhorrent to him, he nonetheless experienced a strong sensation that the woman's soul may have entered his own body, or that it had been waiting by the coffin for him to appear, like a tiny dark bird. Her impassive features were but a mask concealing everything that he had ever thought or imagined. How she had managed to become a part of him was beyond his comprehension. The dark bird of her spirit had absorbed his into its own. He somehow felt the winding sheets about the mummy constraining him even as he tried to draw away.

"Is it possible," he asked, "that we are all victims of a delusion about death? Could it be that each of us is in the throes of drifting toward a more complete life in someone else?"

The scholar had posed a riddle that no mummy, however old, could possibly solve. Nor would the small artifices of coastline or mountain range that I might care to draw on my map be sufficient to describe its peculiar terrain. The earth was simply not big enough to differentiate between an aging scholar's deliberations on the nature of the afterlife and the slow decay of a virgin priestess's remains.

Whoever makes the boat trip over from Venice to this walled hermitage on the island where I live brings all his contradictions with him. Luckily in my cell there lies the possibility for a genuine confluence of ideas, since mine readily mingle with those of my guests. Together we weave what we can from the warp and woof of one another's experience. For the scholar, I suspect that he had unburdened himself of what had been haunting him. He left here knowing that he had contributed important information to the map I had in mind. What he had bestowed on me was the knowledge that the Egyptian priestess's encounter with death, so virginal and yet so prepossessed, had been as abrupt as her encounter with life. I felt that this would turn out to be an interesting headland for us both to visit in our pursuit of respective havens.

NE DAY AN ELDERLY JEW from Rhodes came to visit me. He had lived on the island until the time of the Ottoman seige. After the defeat of the Knights Hospitaller of Saint John of Jerusalem by Sultan Suleiman's forces, he had quit the city in the hope of finding a more congenial spot to live. Now that the Levant had been overrun by the Turk, the ancient wanderings of his people out of Egypt had become for him the hallmark of an exemplary state of mind. He longed to reach a land where milk and honey flowed.

I was struck by the man's interest in meeting me. He had heard my name mentioned by the captain of his ship while en route from Corfu to Venice. He had been informed that at San Michele he would find a monk who might by prepared to hear what he had to say, as the captain assured him that I always had time to listen to the stories of men cast into exile through no fault of their own.

Sitting opposite me on a stool in my cell, the Jew regaled me with snippets of information that he had picked up along the waterfront in Rhodes, in Crete, and in Cypress. It appeared that ever since the collapse of the Latin kingdoms in Palestine all the world had fallen into a state of deep unease. The Crescent had finally triumphed over the Cross; and he, a representative of the Candelabra of the Temple of Solomon, had watched with sinking heart the decline of order in the region.

His eyes spoke of the suffering of his people in the wake of these disruptions. Who but a descendant of those who had initiated the death of Our Lord was better placed to record the demise of His kingdom? After all, his people chose to reject the Living Presence in their midst, the inimitable anguish of existence in the act of transcending itself. For that crime they have suffered, knowing that what they rejected was an incarnation of their own desire to rise above themselves.

The Jew was a cultivated man. He knew his Bible intimately, though of course from the perspective of someone for whom the Book represented only a beginning, not an end. According to him, we can only penetrate the meaning of the Book after it has been taken from us by some catastrophe. I was unsure whether he meant his people's exile from Egypt or his own exile from Rhodes, in the wake of defeat.

As he remarked, "Quitting the place that we love means that we are condemned to inhabit our loss forever."

His discernment captivated me. I felt at times that I was in the company of someone who had stepped back from the normal maelstom of events in order to view his predicament with a more detached eye. He was gazing at the world, and me, as if from a great distance. Separated from his origins as both a man and a Jew, he had discovered in his rootlessness how to inhabit a region of his own mind. He was the first man I had met who had chosen to redeem himself rather than allow another to do so for him. In this sense he was more than a Jew, since the longed-for appearance of the Messiah was not something he anticipated any longer. He had become his own instrument of renewal. Upon his shoulders lay the burden of coping with his alienation in the eyes of the world. As Jew and exile this man seemed to have mastered those twin steeds of defeat and turned them into incomparable warhorses.

It occurred to me while I sat there listening to him that he had made of his Jewishness a badge that he wore with honor. Rather than allow himself to become disheartened by his afflictions, he had chosen to embrace them instead. Probably, too, he had wanted to confer with me because he felt an affinity with what he saw as my isolation. After all, monastery walls have always been there to exclude men such as myself from the world. His solitude and mine he likened to the lonely, intricate pleasure we both felt whenever we chose to embark upon a task, the outcome of which remained uncertain.

"Good friar, my monastery happens to be the world," the elderly Jew announced as I accompanied him to the landing whence his boat back to Venice would shortly embark. About us starlings wheeled in circles, as if searching for a route to take south now that winter was upon us.

"See, they too appear aimless as they begin their quest for a warmer climate," he added, looking upward at the eddying mass of birds.

"It is in us all," he continued, "this desire to experience the kinship that exists between our innermost being and the will that created such a kinship in the first place. As such a desire is realized, we become preoccupied with strange and uncanny aspects in Nature herself. We are almost tempted to regard them as our own moods, our own creations. For my own part, I know that the boundary between myself and Nature sometimes wavers and melts away, so that I can no longer be sure whether what I see with my own eyes springs from outward or inner impressions. An experience such as this is one sure way of discovering how creative we are, and how deeply our soil participates in the perpetual creation of the world. The same invisible divinity is at work in us as it is in Nature. If the outside world were perchance to perish (as it did for me in Rhodes) I know that any one of us would be capable of rebuilding it. I say these things because I believe that mountain and stream, leaf and tree, root and flower, everything that has ever been formed in Nature lies pre-formed within us and springs from the soul, whose essence is eternity. Of course, this essence is beyond all our conceivable knowledge, but we can feel it nevertheless."

Why had the Jew from Rhodes felt the need to say these things? Perhaps he had detected a secularity in me of which even I had not been aware. The Gospels divided us, this much we both knew, and yet our common humanity had managed to overcome any such inhibition.

Like the starlings above we both seemed to be free-wheeling in the air as we gathered together our innermost resolve in order to make that long flight south ourselves. As we embraced on the landing, it struck me that this elderly gentleman, whose ultimate destination not even a trip across the water could resolve (condemned as he was to a life of wandering), was of a most translucent feather indeed.

6

RECEIVED A NOTE one day from an old
friend who had been searching for an unusual icon that had last been seen in a chapel
in Cyprus. Ever since the defeat of the
Knights Hospitaller in Rhodes, Our Lady of Damascus
had found herself wandering the Levant in the footsteps
of the grand master and his entourage. For a time the
order had lived outside Rome, surviving on the goodwill
of others. When Emperor Charles offered the Knights a
haven in Malta, it appeared Our Lady also found a new
and congenial home in this rocky stronghold. Fortunately
for my friend, he finally discovered the icon in a tiny
church there—built, it appears, to proclaim its supreme
gift to the local inhabitants.

I never quite understood why my friend had been so

interested in this icon. It had been painted, after all, in the Byzantine style and bore no relation to the courtly Virgins with which we in Venice are so familiar. From his description of the painting, I gathered that it portrayed the Holy Mother in the Oriental fashion, an image not at all to my personal taste. Perhaps it was its miraculous properties that appealed to him; I don't know. Legend has it that Our Lady of Damascus had saved the Knights on many occasions during their long and fateful encounter with the Saracens.

My friend told me how overjoyed he was to discover the icon in Malta. He spoke of it in glowing terms. He told me also that the people of Malta regarded her as their protector, if only because she had so doggedly defended them in their hour of need. "Her arms are very wide" was the way my friend expressed it to me, hoping that I might understand what he meant.

But his real discovery, he informed me, was the priest responsible for the icon. This man lived alone in a room beside the church, surrounded by a small library of rare and precious tomes. In my friend's words, the priest had "dedicated his life to loving all men, not simply one." It was hard to know whether these were the words of the priest, or whether they were my friend's interpretation of his commitment to the cause of others. In any event, my friend was much taken by this man.

"Father Vitos sees it as his life's mission to care for the icon," my friend wrote. "He informs me that the presence of Our Lady of Damascus in his church invigorates all who come in contact with her. He says this is because she invokes a desire for wisdom, not simply the exercise of one's own desires. He sees this quality as an accretion almost, like a pearl its glister, gathered unto herself during her wanderings in the Levant. My own belief is that Father Vitos has identified himself with the icon's salty pilgrimage. For remarkably Our Lady has an oyster shell imbedded in her forehead. How the icon acquired such a memento in the first place is explained by the story attributed to it, suggesting that a fisherman drew the painting out of the sea in his fishing net with the shell already imbedded. Imagine my surprise when I first set eyes on Our Lady in Father Vitos's church! She stared back at me, the oyster shell protruding from her forehead like a cyclopean eye. No wonder her presence is considered to be so beneficial. This Lady stares at you as if out of the depths of the sea itself."

Now this is the sort of information that makes mapmaking so difficult. If I am to include these facts about Our Lady of Damascus, I need to know where she obtained her unique and pearly decoration. That this icon survived its bout with the sea is a miracle in itself, and is surely worthy of being recorded. I have no way of knowing, however, whether she fell overboard (or was tossed) because of some religious dispute, or whether her swim was precipitated by a need to immerse herself in the sea in emulation of the baptismal rite itself.

Exactitude—it presses upon me like a pestle grinding spices in a mortar. I am bound by the contingencies of how, when, and why things happen. It is clear that neither my friend nor Father Vitos were much concerned by such things when they viewed this remarkable icon, disfigured as it is by the shell of a mollusk. How this should have occurred—how an oyster could have attached itself to a venerable image of Our Lady—was beyond us all. Yet in acquiring this decoration, it seems, the icon had gained in stature. It was no longer a painting that perhaps had been rendered by some obscure Syrian monk long ago, but had become a representation of our Holy Mother that had itself experienced vicissitudes beyond the scope of us humans.

And so a shell, a devout priest, and an icon had been drawn together to form a triplex of veneration. An object, a man, and an anonymous artist's creation had been united in the interest of expressing an idea that was both sublime and immanently accessible. If the people of Malta should regard it as their portector, and for the Hospitallers it had become their rallying point, then surely Our Lady of Damascus had taken upon herself *a life of her own.* She was no longer simply an object of piety and adoration but someone who lived the kind of life that all men aspire to.

I say these things in the light of my own confusion about this matter. If my friend had not mentioned the oyster, and if he had not told me of Father Vitos, I would have been prepared to accept the icon at face value. But now I am not so sure. It seems to me that nature has entered into this dialogue, has understood my struggle, and has replied with a clear voice. The oyster has proclaimed a place of its own in all our hearts. Furthermore, it has broken down the barrier between the anonymous painter and his creation. I am now left with something extra, an added dimension—that of the purest thoughtfulness. I sense that the oyster represents the invisible power of creation attaching itself to what we solemnly believe was created by ourselves.

Probably this is why Father Vitos is so committed to his task. Our Lady of Damascus, for all her aquatic oddity, embodies for him a mystical property that he is powerless to explain. Accordingly, his custodial role now extends to loving all men through her. No wonder my friend was so impressed upon meeting him. Father Vitos is one of those rare men who are tossed up on the shores of the spirit, there to be transformed into objects of veneration themselves. The remote and rocky stronghold of Malta has become, in a sense, his reliquary, housing him in gilded isolation. He has surrounded himself with rare and precious tomes, all of which celebrate his unusual sanctity in a way that few of us could comprehend.

Cartography is a sublime craft. Already I find myself grappling with knowledge that no portolan chart has yet recorded. Sometimes I feel like a floating plate on an astrolabe. Though all my extremities are calibrated to help me determine where I'm going, there are times when a pitching deck renders this impossible. Could it be that I am at the mercy of unseasonal currents, which threaten to drag me off course? Or is it that the oyster-faced icon of Our Lady has managed to lure me toward the same unfathomable abyss to which my friend has found himself such a willing victim?

7

NE DAY I RECEIVED a visit from Signore
Cristoforo Loredan, superintendent of the
secret archives of the Council of Ten in Venice. He had come to enlist my help in translating a series of printed sheets depicting a Turkish map
that had been discovered in the attic by one of his
servants.

According to Signore Loredan, the blocks from which
the sheets were printed had been discovered in a small
wooden cabinet under a pile of disused papers.

"There were several drawers to the cabinet," he explained to me. "In each drawer we found a number of
small wooden blocks engraved with hieroglyphics, which
nobody could decipher. The public printer was asked to
make a copy from these blocks to see what was on them.

When we realized that we had unveiled a map of the world written in the Turkish language, we decided that these sheets must be translated in the interest of state security. Knowing your familiarity with Oriental languages, the Signoria asked me to enlist your help."

I gathered from his statement that he wished me to confirm whether the Turkish map contained information prejudical to the security of Venice. Agreeing to do so, I wasted no time in studying the sheets that he deposited with me for safekeeping. I soon learned that the author of this map, entitled *Perfect and Complete Engraving and Description of the Entire World,* was one Hadji Ahmed, a citizen of Tunis who studied at the mosque of the city of Fez in Morocco, where he learned philosophy, physics, and law. It seems that the man had been captured while returning home to Tunis, and later brought to Venice as a slave. Where he had learned cartography, and who had been his patron in the city, remains a mystery to this day. It may be that Hadji Ahmed had practiced his craft solely at the behest of his anonymous patron, or in the hope of returning with honor to his homeland one day.

The map itself was drawn in the shape of a heart.* Invented by Johann Werner, a mathematician from Nurn-

---

*Known as the cordiform projection, his map of the world was drawn within the outline of a heart. The first major map of this type using a single heart-shaped area to show the entire world was printed in a famous edition of Ptolemy's *Geography,* the Venice edition of 1510. Although Bernadus Sylvanus drew this projection, Johann Werner is considered the originator of this projection, described in his berg, this kind of projection enables the cartographer to show each hemisphere relatively undistorted. It means that the world can be seen from a great height, thus ensuring the viewer a bird's-eye view. It may be that Hadji Ahmed wanted to indicate to his patron how extensive the world really was, or he may have simply wished to emphasize the heights to which a man must climb in order to achieve mastery over himself.

Translation proceeded slowly, since my knowledge of the Turkish language is at best haphazard. Furthermore, Hadji Ahmed's calligraphy tended toward the extremely ornate, necessitating on my part a careful analysis of his words before translating them. The map was surrounded by a series of drawings depicting celestial hemispheres that revealed the principal constellations popular among navigators. There were, or course, numerous references to the infidel religion of Mohammed, which at first I translated with reluctance.

Nonetheless, Hadji Ahmed's turn of mind began to intrigue me. He was particularly attracted to the New World of the Americas. Peru he considered "not a fertile kingdom." Of Mexico he informs us that its principal exports are gold and silver. Of the Europeans, he singles out the

---

work *Libellus de quatuor terrarum orbis in plano figurationibus ab eodem Joanne Vernero novissime compertis et enarratis* (Nurnberg, 1514). Hadji Ahmed copied his map from a cordiform map of this kind printed on a woodcut in Paris in 1536 by the French mathematician Orontius Fineus (1494–1555).

French as a people "respectful of their sovereigns and their arts and sciences, and who have an abundance of wealth and luxury." Legend after legend he had carefully engraved on his map in the hope that all who read it might find themselves better informed.

I was confronted with another man's view of the world and had come in contact with perceptions entirely different from my own. The world as Hadji Ahmed saw it was a potpourri of facts slanted toward the glorification of Allah and the supremacy of Suleiman as the padishah of the Ottomans. What was I to think? Was the man an imposter, or did he possess knowledge that I was not privy to because of my birthright? The more I translated his words, the more I began to believe that neither of us had a hegemony over truth.

His map astonished me with its complexity and the range of information written in its margins. He had located Codfish Land in Labrador, and he acknowledged the existence of cannibals near the mouth of the Amazon. In the gulf separating America from Asia he had noted the island of Simpaga, a place first mentioned by Marco Polo. He also mentioned the existence of a southern continent that he described as "newly found, but not become known in its entirety." This he called the province of Patal.

I was at a loss as to how to deal with all these new facts. Hadji Ahmed had acquired his knowledge from sources with which not even I was familiar. Perhaps he had encountered seafarers in African ports who had ventured to farther parts than most. It seemed that he had gleaned information from the mouths of men who, in their despair, had thrown their humanity into the vast tomb of nature. It may be that these men had abandoned their human nature to its own laws, so that they might leave it behind. Such suppositions ignited my interest in Hadji Ahmed's map even more. I sensed that this obscure Tunisian slave may have witnessed events and heard stories that surpassed even my own.

So here was another fabulist capable of bearing witness to the perambulations of the human heart! It was strange to think that in Hadji Ahmed I had met my counterpart—a man who, like me, wanted to descibe the entire earth by means of his craft. Through the use of words and vague coastlines, the two of us had attempted to give form to something that was not of this world. We had become immersed in the knowledge of other men's experience, experience that we fervently hoped might yet stand the test of time. Were we deluding ourselves? Could we embrace the limits of this world using techniques devised by others?

It was a question I put to myself in the light of Hadji Ahmed's clandestine map. He who had worked for so long in secret, who had taken it upon himself to fashion his vision of the world in the shape of a heart, had managed to convey a sense of purpose in everything that he did. His deft hand, so schooled in the arts of calligraphy and drawing, implied neither a forward nor a backward motion to the earth's orbit, neither an outside nor an inside to its terrestrial form; but rather, a forgetfulness of its shape, as if the world that he saw had becomed demateri-alized as a result of his infinite forbearance.

How could a world like this exist? Were we describing something so entirely inward that its only claim to exis-tence lay in the imagination itself? Hadji Ahmed's map bore little relation to the one I had been working on all these years. It was as if we had been drawing our inspira-tion from two different worlds. While there were similari-ties, of course, in the way we rendered certain facts, the truth was that neither I nor Hadji Ahmed had interpreted common knowledge in the same way. We were as individ-ual in our assessment of what we perceived as the glimmer of lamplight reflected by unquiet waters.

I began to ask myself what else might lie buried in the attic of the secret archives, waiting to be unearthed. A book in code, perhaps, or the diary of some visionary who had been forced to work as a galley slave while his real talent went unheeded? Such thoughts made me realize how fragile is our basis for evaluating the truth. My map, like Hadji Admed's, was only one version of reality. The likelihood of being of any use to anybody remained en-tirely dependent upon its effectiveness as a tool of the imagination. It dawned on me then that the world had to be considered as an elaborate artifice, as the inimitable expression of a will without end.

I don't know what Signore Loredan and the members

of the Signoria expected when they commissioned me to translate Hadji Ahmed's document. Probably they hoped I would discover incriminating information that might assure them of the Grand Turk's continuing designs on Venetian interests throughout the Levant. So far, my researches had proved disappointing. I could find no evidence to suggest that Hadji Ahmed had wanted to do any such thing. Rather, I gained the impression that he had decided not to see either the world or himself as an object of knowledge. In his analysis of what he saw and touched, he embraced the wholeness of things and, through this, the wholeness of himself. He had allowed his inwardness to become a part of his map. Nor could I, a humble observer, remain any more untouched.

8

N UNUSUAL DOCUMENT has fallen into my hands. It came to me by means of a traveler who recently returned from the East. He himself did not journey so far as Cathay, though he believed that the document emanated from that region. It had been given to him as payment of a small debt incurred by a man who traded with the Celestial Empire. The trader thought it might have some value as an object of curiosity to sell to an antiquarian in Venice.

The document detailed the history of the first Christian missionaries to venture into China, as described on a tablet found in the province of Shen-si. This tablet had been erected by a group of Nestorians to commemorate the excellencies of the Christian religion and its widespread propagation in the Middle Kingdom.* Known as Si-gnan-fu, the tablet is considered in certain quarters to be a veritable voice from the dead.

I offered the traveler what I considered to be a fair price for the document. When I sat down to study it, however, I found that it was written both in Syriac characters and in Chinese. Rather oddly, the Syriac characters were arranged in vertical lines, probably as a gesture to its potential readers. In any event, the Chinese portion of the text was headed by the figure of a cross and the title of the monument.

Finally I was able to translate its meaning: *Inscription on stone declaring the introduction and promulgation of the illustrious religion of Ta-tsin in the Middle Kingdom.* Following this was a lauditory chant by a priest of the Church of Ta-tsin. After the chant came twenty-five chapters containing a profession of the Christian faith, an explanation of the ceremonies and observances of the Nestorian

* Nestorianism was an Eastern sect of Christianity founded in the fifth century by Bishop Nestorius of Constantinople. His doctrine emphasized Christ as a "Perfect Man" who had grown up like other men in body and soul. His doctrine implied that Christ possessed two different natures, that of man and God. Denounced by Cyril of Alexandria as a heretic, Nestorius was exiled to the Libyan desert, where he wrote an apologia, the *Book of Heraclides of Damascus,* which sug- gested that his critics had misunderstood him. In it he argued that Christ was the example of a prosopic union, *prosōpon* meaning the external aspect of self-manifestation of the individual. God the Word, he argued, used the manhood of Christ for his self-manifestation, and the manhood therefore became a part of his *prosōpon.* Nestorius's followers remain in Syria and Iraq to this day, where they are known as the Church of the East.

Church, and a general history of the progress of Christianity in China.

The eleventh chapter described the introduction of Christianity in great detail. "In the time of the accomplished Emperor Tai-tsung, whose reign was so brilliant, so flourishing, and who extended far and wide the empire of the dynasty of Tang—in the time of this enlightened monarch, solicitous for the happiness of men, there appeared one of eminent virtue, of the kingdom of Ta-tsin, named Alopen, who, consulting the azure clouds of heaven, and bearing with him the true sacred Scriptures, observed with attention the order of the winds, that he might escape the perils to which he was exposed. He arrived in the ninth year of Ching-kaun in the city of Chang-gnan. The emperor ordered his chief minister, the duke Fang-hiuen-ling, to take with him a military escort, and to meet his visitor at the western suburb in order to escort him into the city. The sacred books, which he had brought, were translated in a hall of the Imperial Palace, and many questions were asked regarding the doctrine in the emperor's private apartments. The doctrine, having been studied profoundly, was judged to be upright and true. So it was ordered that it should be disseminated and taught to the public."

It took me a little time to discover that the alleged Alopen was none other than the Chinese form of the Syriac word *allaha-pna,* meaning "God converts." This must have been the Nestorian word for "missionary." Whoever this anonymous missionary was, he had obviously impressed his Chinese hosts, for they had taken him, his followers, and his doctrine to their hearts. He had been at pains to teach them that self-sacrifice, and a willingness to take risks unto death, are precisely the qualities on which the greatness of the human spirit is based.

I was impressed by the integrity of this document. The monument of Si-gnan-fu stood as a testament to the power of men to disseminate ideals, particularly when they were of an otherworldy dimension. Whether Alopen had been aware of the enduring nature of his actions while he was alive, no one really knows. He has passed into history, a singular figure bearing a Syriac persona impossible to translate into any formal identity other than what he was. In other words, Alopen would remain nameless.

Alopen's anonymity impressed me more than I was prepared to admit. He had traveled to Cathay to propagate ideals, not himself, whereas I had remained here in San Michele di Murano, safe within these monastery walls. To argue that he had merely disseminated a heretical faith and was therefore of no consequence did not justify his dismissal as a charletan. For this saintly nonentity had managed to imbue others with values, a philosophy, and a belief that transcended even himself.

Could it be that this missionary was the embodiment of a new type of man? He had traveled to the limits of the world in order to propagate love and an inner religion. The Chinese were obviously sympathetic to his vision, since they had pronounced his doctrine to be good and true. However heretical either I, or the Holy Catholic Church, might have viewed his teachings to be, clearly its recipients had regarded them more positively. It might be argued that they knew no better, or that their level of knowledge was such that even a heretical doctine was better than none. Whatever Alopen had taught them, he had appealed to something intrinsic in their character that partook of the nature of truth.

If I had any doubts about this document, then these could only be laid at the door of doctrinal orthodoxy, not that of humanity's need to be suffused with a feeling of joy. Alopen's message was clear, almost naïve, given that he consulted clouds and observed the attention of the winds, even though these soothsaying techniques were banned centuries ago by our Holy Church. If I read correctly between the lines, this Nestorian priest radiated a simplicity that the most pagan of peoples were able to recognize for its real worth. It was obvious that the emperor and his minions had embraced Alopen because he represented something different. It followed that while we passionately argue the nature of this "new kind of man" throughout Christendom, and prepare learned dissertations on the subject, some of which often lead to discord among ourselves, Alopen, the anonymous missionary from Syria, had gone to China to affirm that difference in his own person.

I was struck by this contrast. Those who contemplate

the truth from the safety of their garret sometimes lose contact with its essence. True philosophers are those who embark upon a voyage into the unknown, unsure of their destination or whether they might even return. They are like Alopen, missionary to the pagans, in possession of a heretical doctrine the likes of which the world still hungers. Does it matter whether finer points of canonical law are amiss? Such men are more intent on transforming themselves. It is this that radiates from their person, not any set of dogmatic beliefs.

The tablet of Si-gnan-fu, with its parallel texts, was a perfect example of the powers of accommodation and renewal. These lines of vertical Syriac letters were capable of mirroring new insights in a foreign tongue. Through them I was able to envisage the monument rising from the earth in some distant Chinese province, looking for all the world like an obelisk, serene and pointed. Is it any wonder that the people of China revere it as we might an icon? It speaks to them of transcendent values, of age-old virtues that have made the long journey to an emperor's court in order to be received there with honor.

The testament of Si-gnan-fu had been offered to me to recoup a debt. I was grateful that the traveler had chosen to exact its value from me rather than another. Alopen's gift to the people of China lay on the table before me, a reminder of how important a journey to a distant place can be as a mode of discovery. With our paths in life mapped out for all of us, it usually takes the one that leads us away from our goal (to where we are not) to affirm where we should be.

Probably Alopen knew this when he set out on the road to Cathay. He had studied the clouds and listened to the winds: each had told him that his destination would be reached only when he had made of himself a supreme example of his beliefs. In a sense, he *was* the tablet of Signan-fu. He had espoused in parallel text all that he knew, and transformed himself into a living torch to light up the night. The emperor must have been extremely grateful to receive this anonymous Nestorian priest who had bestowed upon his people a crowning thought more voluble than words, more voluble even than the discord of belief.

9

UMORS OF MY WORK are reaching the farthest corners of the world. People who normally would not communicate with me are now doing so in the interest of sharing their knowledge. This is deeply satisfying to me. It means that there are others like myself, living as obscurely as I do, who feel obligated to place before me the fruits of their research, however partial these might turn out to be. We have become brothers in kind, tilling the same field before spring.

I hesitate to use the word *Illuminati* to describe us, but this is a term suggested to me by one of my Mesopotamian correspondents. He discovered it in an obscure text that he found in a monastery library located outside the city of Ninevah. It was written by a Persian monk named

Simon of Taibutheh, one of the last followers of Hippocrates and Galen.* According to the translator of the text,
Simon was regarded as being "head of the theorists" and
a spiritual philosopher of considerable renown. It appeared that my correspondent considered our work closely
aligned to his, hence the use of the word *Illuminati* to
describe us in our endeavors.

Simon's work was difficult to comprehend, being an
odd mixture of mystical insight and scientific observation.
It was the first time I had ever read a text that blended the
style of the rhetoricians of old with the kind of spiritual
insight so familiar to us all. Simon's perspective was
unique to himself. He had allowed the hot stones of the
Persian desert to leaven his thoughts, much like those
placed in a camp oven to make bread rise. It seemed that

---

*Simon of Taibutheh was an
East Syrian writer who lived in the
time of the Patriarch Henanisho.
Little is known about the man, except that he died around 680 A.D.,
but we know that he was a physician as well as a mystic. His sayings
were quoted with respect by the
mystical authors who followed him
(Isaac of Ninevah, for example),
and his teachings exercised some in-
direct influence on the develop-
ment of Islamic Sufism. The epithet
"of Taibutheh" means "of His
grace." It was given to the author
because he had emphasized in his
work the importance of the grace of
God, and the fact that everything

he had acquired was by His grace.

Hippocrates was a celebrated
physician from Cos. He studied
physic under his grandfather, Ne-
brus, and improved himself by
reading the tablets hung up in the
temples of the gods, where each individual had written down the dis-
eases he had suffered and the means
by which he had recovered. Profes-
sionally skillful, he openly admitted
how he cured disorders, while at the
same time acknowledging his fail-
ures. In one instance he confessed
that of forty-two patients entrusted
to his care, only seventeen had recovered! Devoted to his country, he
refused to serve under the Persian

the territory Simon had chosen to investigate was not bound by the limitation of his senses.

According to my Mesopotamian correspondent, Simon's treatise might help to fill in those gaps in my knowledge pertaining to the region of Chaldea and Babylon. He maintained that Simon's insights were a product of this region and therefore needed to be entertained if I were to draw in the physical aspects of such a landscape on my map. Knowledge, he argued, could be acquired only through the combination of the senses of the body and the faculties of the soul. I needed to address these in the work of this philosopher from the East if I were to continue my work.

I labored many long nights in my attempt to understand Simon's thought. Here was a man who valued a balanced relationship between the body and the mind. "As fruit cannot be protected without leaves (since each is in need of the other), so the body needs the soul and the

---

Artaxerxes, who had invited him to join his court. He died at the age of ninety-eight in 361 B.C. free from all disorders of the mind and body. The Hippocratic oath is the basis of modern medical ethics.

Known as Claudius Galenus, Galen was a celebrated physician in the time of Mark Antony and Marcus Aurelius. Born in Pergamon, he applied himself to the study of philosophy, mathematics, and physics. Early in his career he visited the most learned seminaries in Greece and Egypt. In Rome he became famous for his extraordinary cures. His detractors, jealous of his fame, attributed his success to magic. Galen confessed his indebtedness to Hippocrates for his medical knowledge. He wrote over two hundred volumes, the greater part of which were burned in the Temple of Peace in Rome. What remains of his work was published in five volumes in Basil in 1538.

soul the body" is one pertinent remark I came across in the text that served to elucidate his way of thinking. Furthermore, he maintained, "we do not ask for our passions to be destroyed, only that we might be delivered from them." Such remarks made me see the man in a new light. He gloried in the physicality of the world, even as he acknowledged its limitations.

I was reminded of this fact when I read his thoughts on the value of experience as being an important guide in our quest. "A man knows the truth only when he has tried it himself and has not gained it by way of hearsay and reading." He was suggesting that we are obliged to make mistakes if we wish to attain to any degree of knowledge. Conceivably he wanted us to accept that every error we make is one more brick fired in the kiln of grace.

For him, true knowledge was a voluntary freedom divested of all fear. Such a condition Simon called "no-knowledge," whereby everything one assumes to be true, or that one thinks one knows, participates in an essence that is incomprehensible. Knowledge repels itself, just as two lodestones repel one another when compass boxes are brought into proximity.

I was both fascinated and repelled by his belief in no-knowledge. If he were correct, then he was arguing for the abandonment of every fact I believed to be verifiable by way of my senses. Not until I reread his treatise a number of times did I realize that he might have meant something altogether different. "Knowledge of theory is implanted in nature," I read at one point, "and is divided each according to the character of the things that it embraces."

He went on to say, "A part of this knowledge is revealed by reasoning and the construction of logical sentences, and a part of it is apprehended not by words but through the inward silence of the mind. A part of it extends toward visible natures, and another part rises toward natures that are above natural vision."

Simon of Taibutheh trod a delicate line between the spiritual and the corporeal, between the body and the mind. At no time did he wish to raise one above the other. He saw each one of us as the bond of all creation capable of bending our heads in worship, knowing that as we did so the whole of creation bowed its head along with us. By acknowledging how we were conjoined with nature in our every act, Simon wished us to recognize the importance of this conjunction in the form of a sacrament. Nature and man, animal and human—according to him all of these partook of what he called the "rejuvenation of the heart." O discerning man! How your inner vision was illuminated by that mysterious intelligence that you alone attributed to the inward silence of your mind.

For Simon, there really was no difference between what he called the "hidden image and intelligible likeness of the mind," and the intelligible image and likeness of its Creator. There was a connection between natural intelligence and what he termed the "intelligence of the One." Such ideas as these indicated his belief in a form of double vision—one inward looking, the other outward looking. I came across his thoughts on this matter later when he wrote, "Through spiritual theory he will see in his mind spiritually all the visible things that are seen materially by others."

Such a wise man, he insisted, sees materially while striving to investigate in his mind spiritually, using what he called "spiritual theory." He no longer observes various plants like an agriculturalist, nor medicinal roots like a physician, but instead what he sees physically he secretly contemplates in his mind with the use of spiritual theory. This new form of vision enables him to relinquish perplexity in the interest of discernment.

When I tried to envisage what kind of man Simon might have been, I found myself confronting for the first time my own inadequacies. Here was a man who had implemented a new idea of freedom within himself, whereas I was content merely to observe such a transition from afar. My mapmaking had removed me from the fray. I had allowed coastlines and continents to distance me from what I was secretly reluctant to experience. Nor did I have the courage to engage in any battle within myself, since the freedom I knew had not been preceded by the subjection of my will. Unlike the good Simon, it seemed I was still passion's slave.

In my cell overlooking the lagoon here at San Michele, I was made to feel like a bird afraid of quitting its nest. Beyond these enclosed waters, secure as they were against the fury of Adriatic storms, a world of fervor and suffering continued to exist. Men like Simon of Taibutheh still lived in those arid regions of the heart where they engaged in spiritual warfare of a kind that very few of us are able to survive, or indeed contemplate. I was content to gaze at this land from afar rather than embrace it as my own. Somehow I had settled for the *proximity* of life as being enough. Such questions troubled me more than I cared to admit as I pored over the work of this desert father, sent to me by my Mesopotamian correspondent.

What I did ask myself, however, was this: Had my friend deliberately set out to disrupt my cartographic endeavors by presenting me with the work of this rustic? I was enough of a realist to know that my knowledge of the East had to be considerably amended in the light of Simon of Taibutheh's insights. New annotations in the margins would have to be introduced. Erasures would have to be considered. How, for example, would I ever be able to convey the idea of the soul as a cluster of fruit? Or indeed, describe in detail the doctrine of the Three Altars?*

My Mesopotamian correspondent finally provided me

---

*According to Simon of Taibutheh, the doctrine of the Three Altars refers to the mysteries of the Mass, namely the three days of Friday, Saturday, and Sunday. The first altar is the knowledge of works, from which emanate the fulfillment of the commandments. The second altar is knowledge of theory, which is a form of mental exercise. The third altar is the knowledge of hope. It is on this altar that a man sanctifies, glorifies, and praises at all times. Through it he lives, moves, feeds, sleeps, and does everything without interruption.

with the clue when I asked him for his advice. He told me the following story.

"In Ninevah I once knew a wealthy man who had been obsessed with the desire to own musk," he wrote to me. "Not able to find the true article of his choice, he crossed mountains, sailed seas, and traversed land before he reached Cathay, where he presented gifts to the emperor in the hope of receiving a quantity of musk. So impressed was the emperor by this gesture that he allowed the man to cut the musk with his own hands. In due time the man returned to Nineveh and passed it on to his children. They in turn adulterated it with false matter, before handing it on to their descendants. By now the musk had lost all its perfume, as you can imagine.

"In this way," my Mesopotamian correspondent explained, "the ancient fathers desired the truth, trod on life and death, experienced all tribulations, endured all trials, sacrificed themselves, and in time found themselves worthy of the gift of grace. This is what Simon of Taibutheh calls 'spiritual theory.' Unfortunately," he went on, "knowledge of this mystery began to deteriorate as it was handed down, until all that was left lacked real substance. It had lost its perfume in the very act of transmission.

"Perhaps you might wish to draw the journey of this wealthy man from Nineveh on your map," my friend suggested. "But before you do so, consider Simon's treatise as the unadulterated musk that he received after visiting the emperor. If you transcribe the contours of his message correctly, then there is a prospect of retaining its essence for others to experience. I hope this suggestion will help you with your endeavors," he concluded.

I was grateful for my friend's advice. He too must have been deeply affected by Simon of Taibutheh's thought. Perhaps it was he who had been the wealthy traveler who visited the emperor's court in Cathay. Who knows? Disguising his identity might have been one way of emphasizing his message.

I began to recognize one important point. As Illuminati, my friend and I were deeply committed to charting the course of wayfarers such as Simon of Taibutheh. Their journey to regions beyond that of normal concourse could be likened to those of wealthy men who presented themselves at the court of emperors in the hope of receiving the musk of no-knowledge. Was this not, after all, what Simon meant when he spoke of the intelligence of the One?

IO

HE CREATION OF MY MAP has assumed a dimension that was not a part of my initial considerations, though of course I had expected the information I received to be contradictory at times. This was bound to happen when one is gathering facts that cannot be verified. But I had not expected to receive so much *meditative* knowledge. Obviously my correspondents wished to convey only what they felt was important to the completion of my task.

The idea that knowledge might embody feelings, as much as observation, certainly left me in a quandary. Whenever I opened various missives sent to me from afar, or heard the personal reflections imparted to me by merchants and adventurers who visited me at San Michele, I was struck by the realization that their observations were not independent at all. Rather, they were affected by sentiments that each of them held to be an expression of himself. In the end, the world they offered me was reflected through them.

I was left with the lingering doubt whether I was acquiring a correct picture of the world. Could it be that I had been misinformed? Perhaps the world was actually different from the one I had begun to perceive. Every man who had ever lived became a contributor to the evolution of the earth, since his observations were a part of its growth. The world was thus a place entirely contructed from thought, ever changing, constantly renewing itself through the process of mankind's pondering its reality for themselves.

It led me to the idea of fashioning a map that would defy every category and genre. It would be a map that would contain them all; a map hard to define, yet because of this lack of definition, a map that would begin to define itself more precisely. Nor would it be one designed to espouse any particular policy or persuasion. Rather, I wanted my map to show the earth in the sky, and the sky on earth; a map that would act as the prototype for all maps scattered in space and in time. It would be a device by which the world could surrender itself in fragments to the open, inquisitive gaze of everyone. I fondly hoped that such a map would preside over the birth of another map, and then another.

All my early work had been but a preparation; every

observation brought to my attention but the beginning of a process of recognition. Though I was seeing the world through the gaze of others, I somehow believed that the world they had seen, I had seen also. In the act of recording their experiences I was translating for them what had been for them indecipherable. The things they had observed were phenomena only; what I attempted to inscribe onto my map was the transformation of their observations into that uncluttered grace we find in all living relationships.

My map had become a sort of catechism. Questions and answers pervaded the great free space that was the world. The interior of Africa, peopled by homunculi and hairy-bodied men, posed a riddle about what might be considered normal in the first place. Knowing there may be rocs flying about clutching elephants in their talons was enough to convince me that there was no rhyme or reason to the way the earth expressed itself.

Although I had appointed myself its unofficial cartographer, I had no way of knowing whether I was reflecting the earth's existence or my own. I began to suspect that the world and I were living lives that were out of kilter in some way. When we did happen to meet in an act of mutual recognition, it was as if we had met one another for the first time. Only then could my sensibility partake of another. I finally realized that I do not live alone, but in the bosom of what made me.

Of course, I had hoped I might bring to bear a level of

clarity to my activities. I wanted to see things differently. I wanted each annotation on my map to represent the reconstruction of a more complete personal world. Both the roc and its burden were aspects of myself. I too flew beyond the margins of my world, weighed down by an ancient grief. Yet somehow I had managed to remain in the air like the roc. The incongruity of that which I held on to (namely, the elephant) had not dragged me down to earth. I could still fly, in spite of what I considered to be an incomparable load.

This is the world I have chosen to describe: an old earth populated by strange wonders and mysterious creatures. When I see the boat arrive at the landing below, I begin to wonder who is coming ashore to offer me what he has witnessed in his wanderings. Life lays bare his beginnings even as he steps ashore and rearranges his cloak. Under it a measure of truth lies concealed like a sword.

Patience. I need as much of it as I can muster. The world may seem to be at my doorstep (is that an emissary from the Vatican I see below, stepping ashore with a packet under his arm?), but it too is an illusion. I must be careful not to assume that all I hear fully renders what is out there, on the far side of some mountain range, or by the shores of a remote harbor.

Errors of understanding go hand in hand with recognition: this I now know to be true. Each man brings to me impressions of his world, believing that he possesses it exclusively. When he encounters a sacred well where saints bathe, then of course he is keen to inform me of its uniqueness. Am I to inform him that such a detail may have been witnessed in other parts of the world by other men? No, of course not. I cannot break the spell of discovery, because it alone sustains him when he needs it most.

In a way, then, I remain imprisoned in the gilded solitude which is San Michele, unsure of my own motives, while beyond it the world continues to exist as a figment only, a shadowy expression of itself. Men may of course view it and believe they have seen it in its entirety, but they are inevitably deceived. What they see is ultimately determined by what limits them from viewing its wholeness. The level of their awareness prevents them from recognizing the invisibility of its substance.

All this leaves me in a quandary. I have become a prisoner of knowledge, having been inundated by too many facts. People are impressing upon me what they know, little realizing how much their experience is changing me. It is as if I have become a victim of their desire to affirm the uniqueness of their vision. Who I am becomes meaningless in the wake of their need to account for their own addiction to the principle of surprise. I ask myself whether this is how the world changes, how it realizes itself anew—not as a shifting planet in the heavens, but as a conjunction of thought in space.

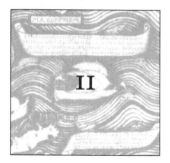

II

s I suspected, an emissary from the Vatican has come ashore to converse with me. News has reached His Holiness the Pope of my project, and accordingly he has instructed his archivists to make available certain documents he felt might prove to be of value in my research.

Having received visits from numerous foreign legates over the centuries, it was inevitable that the Vatican might find itself the beneficiary of their distant observations. Whether it might be a report on the travels of three princes from Serendip, or the journey of Raban Sawma from Arghon* pleading for Europe's help in reclaiming

---

*Raban Sawma was the envoy of a remote Eastern king known as Arghon. In 1285 he visited Naples, Rome, Paris, and Bordeaux, attempting to persuade European monarchs to join with Arghon and take Jerusalem from the Saracens.

Jerusalem, the Vatican archives are a rich hoard of accumulated knowledge about the world.

One of the items the Vatican emissary passed on to me that did catch my eye was a report by a Franciscan monk, Johannes de Plano Carpini, detailing the events of his journey to the country of the Tartars.* His observations on this remote and hostile people proved to be invaluable. Through his eyes, I was able to enter the streets of Genghis Khan's capital, Karakorum, and share with him my first drink of cosmos.

---

*Giovanni da Pian del Carpini was a Franciscan friar appointed by Pope Innocent IV to travel to the court of the Mongols in an attempt to enlist their friendship. In his sixties when he departed, he arrived in Karakorum in the summer of 1246, in time for the coronation of the Grand Khan Güyük. He described this Oriental fantasy of tents and pavilions, richly garbed Mongol chieftains and ambassadors, in his famous *Liber Tartarorum,* one of the gems of medieval literature. Though he did not convert the khan to Christianity, he did manage to meet the man, who was surrounded by "the noise of music, and was bowed to, or honored with fair wands, having purple wool on the tops of them." The pope's document that he presented is an interesting exercise in cultural arrogance. It read, "You must come yourself at the head of all your kings and prove to us your fealty and allegiance. And if you disregard the command of God and disobey our instructions, we shall look upon you as our enemy." The great khan's reply amply reflects the Mongol's dismay at Pope Innocent's intolerance: "You inhabitants of the western lands consider yourselves alone to be Christians and despise us. How then do you know who is worthy in the sight of God to partake of His mercy? When you say to yourselves, 'I am a Christian, I pray to God and serve Him, and I hate the others,' how do you know whom God considers righteous and to whom He will show His mercy?" Giovanni reached Kiev on his return journey in June 1247, seven years before Marco Polo was born, thus completing the first recorded journey by a European to the court of the Mongols.

I will not pretend that such a beverage did not intrigue me. According to Fra Johannes, cosmos was made from mare's milk in the following manner. A rope was attached to two posts firmly placed in the ground. Foals of mares designated for milking were then tied to the rope so that the mares might stand by their offspring. A man would allow the foal to suckle for a short while, before removing the animal and milking the mare without her knowledge.

The milk was later placed in a large bladder or bag and beaten with a hollow club whose head looked like that of a man's. In time the milk began to boil like new wine, its taste becoming sour. When the taste was so sharp that it rasped the tongue and the liquid had congealed into butter, it was considered to be at its best. Those who have tasted cosmos say that it leaves a taste like almonds. "A marvelous sweet and wholesome liquor," Fra Johannes called it, "which alleviates the need for passing urine."

But I digress. Fra Johannes and his associate, a Pole by the name of Benedict, had been sent by Pope Innocent to the court of the Tartars in order to exhort them to give up their bloody slaughter of mankind and to receive the Christian faith. They traveled on horseback from Lyons down the Dnieper and across Russia, reaching the country of the Kirghiz by way of Tashkent and the Altai Mountains. They crossed deserts and forded rivers. They met up with warriors and bandits along the way. Summer storms and winter blizzards hindered their progress at every turn. Only a firm belief in their ultimate purpose enabled them to reach the land of the Tartars, where they presented the Pope's petition to the Great Khan himself.

"These people have strange beliefs," Fra Johannes wrote. "One is to thrust a knife into the fire, or cut with their hatchet near a fire. By this means, they hope to take the power of the fire unto themselves. Another is to lean upon their whip before they beat their horses, and to touch arrows with their whips before they launch them at their enemy.

"Fire, it seems," added the good friar, "figures large in all their activity. Men who wish to enter their tabernacles must pass between two fires, as does any gift granted by prince or ambassador. This act of purification renders all things purged of poison or other mischief."

I was impressed by the calmness in which Fra Johannes made his observations. I sensed in him a conviction that the world was indeed ordered, in spite of the strange things he had witnessed. It was as if he were observing things from afar, perhaps elevated by the potency of the cosmos he had so clearly enjoyed while among the Tartars. This drink, which intimates the universe, certainly drew forth from him impressions that others might have passed over as insignificant.

How else can one judge his pronouncement on a certain people who lived underground because they could not bear the noise of the sun rising? According to Fra Johannes, such a people had emerged from the earth to attack Genghis Khan and his company. They would have overrun his men had it not been for the dreadful sound of the sun. So loud was it that they were forced to lie with one ear to the ground and the other stopped by their hand, for fear of dying. The noise of sunrise enabled Genghis Khan's men to rout their attackers before they had been overcome themselves.

Or consider the one-eyed monsters they met in desert places, known as Cyclopedes. With one arm and one hand protruding from their breasts, and possessing only one foot, these men used to bend a bow in tandem. Faster than a horse, they either hopped along the ground or cartwheeled in accordance with their wont.

He spoke also of the people of Burithabeth, who appeared to be largely made up of women. When asked where their menfolk might be, he was informed by the women that they had been exiled to the far side of a river because of their appearance. They resembled dogs more than they did men, having acquired this characteristic through the habit of swimming in the water during winter and then wallowing in the dust. Their frozen skins, caked hard with mud, made them look like canines. Such a mode of protection successfully shielded them against the spears and arrows of their enemies. When they attacked the Tartars they wounded them with their teeth. The Tartars themselves often spoke of either a brother or father being "slain by dogs."

All this information left my curiosity unsated. The cool eye of Fra Johannes made real a world of peoples little given to the habits of civilized men. Overrefinement, luxury, scepticism, and weariness of spirit had not taken root among the arid steppes of Asia or among the tents of the nomads he met. Drinking in the universe (in the guise of mare's milk) was still a heady potion for these wild and untrammeled peoples.

"Neither thieves nor robbers, the Tartars put no faith in amassing great riches," Fra Johannes wrote. "Locks and bars on windows are unknown. If a beast from the herd goes astray, the finder invariably returns it to its owner. Courtesy mixed with cruelty seems to be a characteristic of theirs. Riding, they are capable of enduring extreme cold and heat. For them superfluity enslaves, and they are always on guard against drunkenness and insolence. Is it any wonder that they have become a scourge upon the peoples of Europe, who fear them as they do the plague? When they knock at the door we know they have come to relieve us of our excesses."

Fra Johannes's report, though ancient in itself, celebrates the immediacy of the moment. In his world I am among people who care little for the comforts of city life. For them, the desert and wild places represent not death but a test of life. It gives them the strength to fight against the militancy of death. Nor are they victims of a need to secure a measure of refinement; rather, they seek out danger in the hope that it will intensify their struggle to live.

Fra Johannes's report on the country of the Tartars suggests that the world is as polyphonic as the music of High

Mass. All the echoes of men's aspiration are in counterpoint. Whether it is cosmos we drink in or the sound of the sun, each draft leaves us feeling more intimately at one with ourselves. What wisdom is acquired during the course of a life is a result of the mind's tenderness toward the heart.

Fra Johannes met up with men who despised all sense of order. Men who subject their bodies to the rigor of frozen rivers, then wallow in dust so they look like dogs, obviously see animality and asceticism as much the same. Wild men exiled by their women take on an aura of invincibility when they go into battle against heavy odds. They can defeat even the cruellest of men, however courteous their enemy might be at times. Discord governs their actions. Animality and asceticsm, cruelty and courtesy—these rub against one another and so cause a spark that enflames their bodies into an act of rebellion, whereby they accept being at odds with themselves as a true measure of their freedom.

The Cyclopedes knew this also, it seems, when they made their physical disability into their strength. Drawing a bow in tandem or cartwheeling in flight meant that they were able to make their odd union work, in spite of their obvious disadvantage. It appeared also that the one bold hand protruding from their breast pointed to a sense of the infinite beyond rather than any visible limitation.

Even as I muse on these things, across the water I hear the bell towers of Venice tolling. They remind me that at no moment are we truly absent from ourselves. Listening to them, I know they are drawing me back from the precipice. Yet I feel constrained. I sometimes wish I might exercise the courage to travel beyond myself, to journey like Fra Johannes into a wilderness of strange creatures in order to petition the Great Khan himself. As a result of his adventure he was able to drink cosmos, and so experience a genuine transformation that he had probably never experienced before.

Ah, it is a condition I long for. I who have made this secure place my fortress. Unlike the Cyclopedes, no gesture to reach beyond this world and embrace the imaginary ever issues forth from my breast. I cannot cartwheel through space. Rather, I am pinioned by a fear of those things that do not conform to my sense of order. It's true, I have never heard the sound of the sun echoing in my ears, not once.

What is wrong? Am I not of the same world as those warriors who wallow in mud? Have I not felt the barb of exile? Perhaps I need to pass between two fires and become purified. Yet all this wildness, this test of life, troubles me with its intensity. There is so much that I must give up if I am to hear again the deep ancestral voice of soul calling to soul.

Outside, I watch the last light of day lingering on the surface of the lagoon. The stones in my cell seem to ache as their warmth begins to dissipate. I hear my fellow monks shuffling along corridors toward evening service, while on my desk lie the words of one like myself, a way-farer to the world's corners. Tonight in chapel I must offer up a prayer in His name, calling upon Him to grant me the gift of courage also. Fra Johannes's observations have already alerted me to a pleasure that may be derived from the tart flavor of almonds, a flavor derived not only from mare's milk but from the taste of asceticism mingled with disorder.

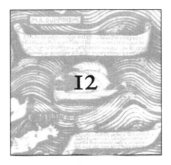

12

MONG THE PAPERS left with me by the papal legate was the journal of another wandering friar, William of Rubrouck. He had also made a journey to the land of the Tartars at the request of King Louis of France. His commission was to seek out the legendary Prester John, said to live among the Keriat peoples. For centuries there has been a desire to meet with this fabled Christian prince of the East in the hope of forming an alliance. Conquering the Saracen and retaking Jerusalem was said to be a dream of Prester John's, as it was for King Louis.*

---

*Louis IX was one of the early patrons of the crusading movement. According to Walter Map, he was a man of lofty humility and mild self-assurance, the epitome of France during the medieval period. Reflect-

William's journey may have been in response to a letter received by the then Emperor Manuel Comnenus of the Byzantines, which subsequently went the rounds of most European courts, such was the curiosity it aroused.* In it Prester John acknowledged his allegiance to our Lord Jesus Christ while bestowing his greetings on the emperor. He also suggested that any mission sent to his kingdom would be met with the cordiality and respect that it deserved.

"If you wish to come to our kingdom," Prester John announced, "we will place you in the highest and most exalted position in our stronghold, and you may freely partake of all that we possess. Should you desire to return, you shall go laden with treasures. If indeed you wish to know wherein consists our great power, then believe without doubting that I, Prester John, who reign supreme, exceed in riches, virtue, and power all creatures who dwell under heaven. I have made a vow to visit the sepulchre of Our Lord with a very great army, as befits the glory of Our Majesty.

:ocuocuocuocuocuoci

ing on the different kinds of wealth possessed by various rulers, he said, "Few men can have everything. The kings of the Indies are rich in precious stones and rare beasts; the emperor of Byzantium and the king of Sicily are rich in gold and silk; the German emperor has no gold or silk or other luxuries. Your lord, the king of England, has everything—men, horses, gold, silks, gems, wild beasts—everything. We in France have nothing: only bread and wine and joy."

*Manuel I Comnenus (c. 1122–80) presided over the scourge of the Crusades on Eastern Christendom. A brilliant ruler, soldier, and diplomat, he was eventually crushed by the Seljuq Turks in Asia Minor, which in turn paved the way for the occupation of the Byzantine capital by the Latins in 1204.

"Furthermore," the king added, "our magnificence dominates the Three Indias, and extends to farthest India, where the body of Saint Thomas the Apostle rests. It reaches through the desert toward the place of the rising sun and continues through the valley of deserted Babylon, close by the Tower of Babel.

"In our territories are found elephants, camels, and almost every other kind of beast under heaven. Honey flows in our land, and milk everywhere abounds. In one of our territories no poison can do harm and no noisy frogs croak, no scorpions are there, and no serpent creeps through the grass.

"In one of the heathen provinces flows a river called Physon, which, emerging from Paradise, winds through the entire province. In it are found emeralds, sapphires, carbuncles, topazes, onyxes, beryls, sardonyxes, and many other precious stones.

"In another of our provinces are worms, which in our tongue we call salamanders.* These worms can live only in fire and make a skin around themselves as the silkworm

---

*In popular medieval bestiaries the salamander symbolized the fire of the alchemists. It was supposed to be of itself the nature of fire, a fiery essence known as "Salamandrine essence." According to Paracelsus, Salamandrini was a man or spirit of fire, a fiery being. Because it had proved its incorruptibility in fire, such a creature enjoyed a particularly long life. The salamander was also known as the "incorrupt-ible sulfur" said to promote a more rarified spiritual condition in the alchemist. Nicolas Flamel, a French alchemist of the fourteenth century, likened the salamander to the hermetic vessel in which alchemists brewed their spiritual potion, the elixir of eternal life. He remarked, "How often did I see them [the achemists] overcome with joy at my understanding, how affectionately they kissed me, for the true grasp of

does. The skin is carefully spun by the ladies of the palace, from which cloth for common use is woven. When we wish to wash the garments fashioned from the cloth, we put them into fire, and they come forth fresh and clean.

"We also possess a stone of great medicinal virtue, capable of curing Christians and would-be Christians alike. In the stone there is a cavity shaped like a giant mussel shell, in which the water is always four inches deep. The sacred water is cared for by two holy men. They ask all visitors to the stone whether they are Christians or not, before they are given permission to take off their clothes and climb into the shell. When they have done this three times, the water invariably returns to its normal height. Everyone who enters the shell comes forth fully cured.

"Flattery finds no favor in our land, nor are there any lies. There is no strife among us. Our people have an abundance of wealth. Our horses, however, are few and wretched. I believe there is none to equal us in wealth and numbers of people.

"The palace in which our sublimity lives is modeled on the building erected for King Gundafor by the Apostle Thomas.* The roof is of ebony that cannot be injured by

ιοειιοειιοειιοειιοειιοει

the ambiguities of their paradoxical teaching came easily to my mind. How often did their pleasure in the wonderful discoveries I made concerning the abstruse doctrines of the ancients move them to reveal unto my eyes and fingers the Hermetic vessel, the salamander, the full moon, and the rising sun."

*Saint Thomas, the apostle who doubted Christ's resurrection, was the traditional founder of Indian fire. At the extremities, above the gables, are two golden apples, in which are set two carbuncles, so that the gold shines by day and the carbuncles shine by night. The greater gates of the palace are of sardonyx inlaid with the horn of the serpent known as *cerastes,* so that none may enter with poison. Our court dines at tables made of gold and amethyst, with ivory columns supporting them.

"In front of the palace is a square where we watch judicial trials by combat. The square is paved with onyx so that the fighters' courage may be increased by virtue of the stone. No light burns in our palace that is not fed by balsam. The chamber in which our sublimity reposes is marvelously bedecked in gold and all manner of precious stones. But whenever onyx is used as an ornament, four carnelians are set about it so that the evil virtue of the onyx may be tempered. Our bed is of sapphire in accordance with the virtue of chastity, which this gem has in abundance. We possess the most

---

Christianity. His career is highlighted in the apocryphal *Acts of Thomas,* which was probably composed in the city of Edessa in the third century. On his arrival in India, Thomas was asked by King Gundafor to build him a new palace. Thomas gave the money designated for the task to the poor and needy, thus earning the king's ire. Gundafor's brother Gad, distressed by Thomas's actions, took to his bed and died of chagrin. On his journey heavenward he beheld a magnificent palace, and he asked the name of its owner. He was told that the palace belonged to his brother, and that the architect was none other than Thomas. Gad asked permission to return to the world to inform his brother of the splendid palace that awaited him in the heavenly realms. This request was granted, and after hearing the story of the celestial palace from Gad, Gundafor urged Thomas to receive him into Christianity.

beautiful women, but they approach us only four times in the year, and then solely for the procreation of sons.

"If you ask us how it is that the Creator of all things," Prester John concluded, "having made us the most supreme and the most glorious over all mortals, does not give us a higher title than that of presbyter or priest, let not your wisdom be surprised on this account, for here is the reason. At our court we have many ministers who are of higher dignity than ourselves in the Church, and of greater standing in divine office. Furthermore, in our household a steward can be a patriarch and a king, a butler can be an archbishop and a king, a chamberlain can be a bishop and a king, a marshall can be a king and an archbishop, our chief cook a king and an abbot. It does not seem proper that Our Majesty assume such names, or be distinguished by those titles with which our palace overflows. Therefore, to show our great humility, we choose to be called by a lesser name and to assume an inferior rank. If you can count the stars in the sky and the sands of the sea, you will be able to judge for yourself the vastness of our realm and power."

Such a letter must have aroused a good deal of curiosity among the courts of Europe when it first appeared. William's journey at the behest of King Louis may well have been to confirm whether this ideal kingdom really did exist. The realization that Prester John might have ruled over heaven on earth, complete with its sapphires, virtues, and titular inversions, must have been a tempting prospect for men so long in the grip of controversy and weary from constant warfare. No man of worth could pass up the opportunity to sit at the feet of a perfect ruler, whether he were a king or a priest.

William proceeded to the country of the Tarters by a slightly different route from that of his predecessor, Johannes de Plano Carpini. He set sail from Acre in the Holy Land to the port of Kaffa in the Black Sea. From there he journeyed overland across the steppes, and thence veered northeast at Lake Balkhash, where he traversed the Altai Mountains in the region of the Naiman peoples.

His journal is littered with observations of what he saw en route. Whether he is commenting on drinking from a cup fashioned from the crooked horn of a beast known as an artak or hawking in the gorges of Persia, rarely does William not enlighten his readers. His world is one where every incident infatuates to the point where I begin to ask myself whether these might be the aftertaste of lies.

I do not know why I say this, except that William's journey had been made in response to a vision. Prester John's kingdom made up of battlefields in onyx bespoke some image that he obviously found difficult to dismiss. It seems he had become the handmaid of an expectation hard to fulfill, for he had perceived in Prester John's unusual approach to government a progressive sense of diminution, rising, as if in tiers, all the way to a summit. Who but an Oriental potentate could create for his people such a magnificent enclave out of the thirsty stones of a desert?

Prester John's letter to the emperor of the Byzantines titillates with its extravagant claims. Our sublimity's munificence dominates not only the Three Indias but also what constitutes an interior terrain. For the king-priest who rejects all need of a title, yet lives on in an elevated state, must in himself prefigure a renewed confidence in the value of being human. Though he adores precious stones, these remain distant from his presence, insofar as he wishes to achieve a pure state of independence. Prester John is moved more by a sense of enlarged life than by those treasures that magnify him by way of their illusory qualities.

There is no kingdom more replete with anguish than one that relies on the fealty of inferior ideals. Prester John lives in a dream. He imagines a perfect state over which he reigns. His bed is tapestried in chastity, and his wives bear only virtuous sons. All illness is transient in the face of holy men and self-leveling mussel shells. A kind of self-perpetuating innocence is abroad that is capable of silencing frogs and ensuring a continual flow of milk and honey.

Indeed, some principle of excellence is at work within his realm that transcends the ruling power of the king. He is not its perpetrator but its servant. Hence his wish to be addressed by the humble title of presbyter rather than one that suggests his right to order reality in accordance with his will.

Are these not the wild rantings of someone afflicted by excessive vapors? Fra Mauro, I sometimes tell myself, this map is debilitating your mind. You have become addicted to the observations of men. You are not your own man but a composite of others. You allow them to taunt you with topazes, believing that these gems are the stuff of a rich inner life. Like William of Rubrouck, you trudge across unknown country, seeking word of some mystical realm that others have heard of but so far have not visited themselves. You tell yourself that somewhere a kingdom of bliss is bound to exist, though in what form it is hard to tell. Furthermore, you argue that Prester John's decription is obviously a complete fabrication rendered in the interest of perpetuating a lie. For no man, you tell yourself, could possibly wear clothes woven from the skin of salamanders and survive an ordeal by fire.

Yet for all that, I am reluctant to denounce Prester John as a hoax. According to William's report, one day he met a shepherd in Cathay who told him of a Christian king lording it over the people of Nayman. "They called him King John, and reported ten times more of him than was true," William wrote. "His people blaze abroad great rumors, and report on just nothing." As far as William was concerned, the shepherd's story confirmed what he already suspected: that the legend of Prester John had grown larger the farther west it had roamed.

The presence of his letter in the Vatican archives only served to emphasize the existence of an imagined kingdom. That it had continued to live on in men's minds for so many centuries affirms at least something about the human predicament: that people long for a kingdom of God. Nor was I such a fool for believing in its hoped-for existence. King Louis had believed in it, and so had William at the onset of his journey. Between them, king and friar had made a pact with distance and vicissitudes in the hope of discovering their prototype of an ideal prince. They wanted to know whether it were possible for someone, prince or pauper, to elevate himself above the ordinary ruck of existence.

Prester John's realm lay on no known trade route. Rather, he had set up his kingdom in the minds of travelers and pilgrims alike. These men were like me. What I acted out on paper in the confines of my study, they chose to pursue to the ends of the earth. It did not occur to them that such a world was largely of their own making. The prospect of gazing upon tables of gold inlaid with gemstones was more than enough to keep them going. Had not Prester John informed them that he would place them in the most exalted position, should they choose to visit him? They longed to become subjects of his excess, the bounty to which he was ultimately indifferent. They longed to become his slaves.

Prester John reigned over a kingdom of the invisible. He lived in a palace that was everywhere and nowhere at the same time. Whoever visited him became exalted, in keeping with his promise. My own wish, of course, was to transcribe the location of his kingdom on my map. I knew it would be impossible. This man, who robed himself in salamander's skin in order to remain immune from fire, knew how to rise from his own ashes. He was a godlike being, utterly incorruptible, in league with the river of life as he wound through province after province, bestowing upon all the gift of knowledge.

It was enough for William and myself to marvel at the

power of his story. In the end, it was to the invisible presence of Prester John that we must ultimately make our act of obeisance, aware that his palace was built from much more than golden apples and carbuncles. It was built of dreams.

NE AFTERNOON I RECEIVED a visit from a merchant who had recently returned from Persia. I say merchant because he informed me that he bought and sold silks and spices that he obtained in the bazaars of the Orient. My initial impression of the man after hearing him talk was that he dealt in goods more exotic than those normally attributed to commerce.

He spoke fluent Greek, though with a pronounced Levantine accent. Perhaps he had originally come from one of the Greek communities in Asia Minor. Nor did he willingly volunteer any information about his homeland. I gained the impression that his office was under his cloak, and his place of residence the cabin of a ship. Grave and somewhat considered in his opinions, he rendered his thoughts in the manner of one long used to meditating while riding a camel toward some distant city.

The information he passed on to me in the solitude of my study was in sharp contrast to his profession. It was clear that certain events he had witnessed in the past had affected him profoundly. His encounter with the Yazidis, or Devil worshipers of Mosul, for example, which he mentioned to me during our conversation, had wrought a considerable change in his beliefs. He told me that the new sense of worth that he had acquired after meeting with the emir of the Yazidis had enabled him to take out a fresh lease on life.

"It happened while I was crossing a remote region of Sheikhan," he related to me. "A sandstorm forced our caravan to take refuge in the castle of Ba-Idri, some distance from Al-Qosh. I had not imagined at this point that the man who came forward to offer us a haven for the night was the head of an obscure sect that worshiped Satan.*

"In appearance Said Beg, the emir of the Yazidis, was tall and extremely slim. A long tapering black beard all but obscured his face. He looked older than he really was,

---

*According to the Byzantine commentator Michael Constantine Psellus (1018–1078), there was a common conception among the Euchites that Satan was the first-born son of God, and that Christ was the second. According to such a view, Satan must be considered as the dark chthonic half of the Christian Godhead. Nor is he simply evil as such, but is rather good and evil, or a system of higher powers in the lower. Such a totalization of Christ and Satan must have been in the minds of the Yazidis when they made the serpent a symbol of divine possibility. It was not evil that they worshiped, but rather the reintegration of the day into the night.

and his mournful expression gave him a faintly sinister look. He wore baggy breeches embroidered in black silk, and a black jacket similarly embroidered. On his head he secured his white coverlet with a black headband. His boots were black also. Everything about the man befitted someone who called himself the lord of the votaries of Satan.

" 'My people have worshiped the Peacock Angel, known to us as Malak Taus, since the time of the Assyrians,' Said Beg informed me as we ate our repast from copper trays.

" 'Do you believe this being to be the Devil?' I asked him.

The emir nodded.

" 'No one pronounces his true name without running the risk of death,' he remarked.

"It became evident to me that this obscure cult originated among the sun worshipers of ancient times, for one of their practices was to adore the rising sun and to kiss the spot where the first rays of dawn appear. Their doctrine was a mixture of Christian, Jewish, and Mohammedan belief. They accepted the divinity of Christ, though they believe His reign will not come until after the Devil's is over. They regard the Old and New Testaments, as well as the Koran, as inspired tomes. They circumcise like the Muslims, baptize like Christians, and abstain from unclean foods like the Jews. I gained the impression that

Malak Taus is made up of a combination of Moses, Jesus, and Mohammed!

"According to Said Beg, the Yazidis possess their own sacred writings," the merchant continued. "In the Black Writing (*Kitab al-Aswad*) and the Book of Revelations (*Kitab al-Jilwah*), which he showed me, a series of proclamations set forth the might and powers of Satan to his followers. 'I am, I am, and I shall be unto the end of time, ruling over all creatures and ordering the affairs and deeds of those who are under my sway,' Satan proclaims in one part that he translated for me.

"What surprised me most, however, was the identity of their principal saint, Sheikh Adi, a Kurdish gardener of the twelfth century. It appears that Adi was a murderer. He, along with his sons, had been a steward in a nearby Nestorian monastery. Revolting against their employers one day, they forced the holy men to perform menial tasks in the convent until they decided to murder them. It seems that Said Beg, the hereditary emir of the Yazidis and my host that evening, was the descendant of these monk-assassins, an honor that did not at all seem to perturb him.

"As if to assure me of the veracity of his beliefs, Said Beg invited me to accompany him on the following day to the shrine of Sheikh Adi. Thankfully the storm had abated, but my caravan was not yet ready to depart. And so, in the company of his retainers, we journeyed on horseback for three hours until we reached the shrine. It lay in a pleasant valley filled with groves of walnuts, figs, and pistachios. Poplars grew beside a nearby stream. Meanwhile, the shrine lay hidden in a bower of giant mulberry trees. Here, in the forecourt of the Temple of the Sun, a remarkable and, may I say, disturbing sight met my gaze.

"Amid all this beauty, this paradisiacal valley, dear friar, I encountered a shiny black serpent carved into the wall beside the entrance to the shrine. I was at once reminded that as idyllic as the valley seemed, I was in the Devil's lair. The charm of spring on that day was at once darkened by a cloud of evil.

"When I asked Said Beg why the shrine was not the object of raids by the local Kurdish people between pilgrimage seasons, he informed me that such people dared not set foot inside the sanctuary. The reason he gave was their fear of the demonic power of Malak Taus. The Prince of Darkness, you see, has the power to destroy all who oppose him."

The merchant's decription of the followers of Satan came as a surprise. His very anonymity gave his story an authenticity I would not have normally granted such an account if it had been presented to me in the form of a traveler's journal. Perhaps this is why he had wanted to visit me in person. He knew that an encounter with the followers of the Devil might sound inconceivable in the form of a literary expression; but as an oral account, accompanied by all the gravity of personal experience, his report would have to be taken more seriously.

Superficially, his encounter with a people whose beliefs were totally opposed to those of normal civilized beings seemed like a rebuke. That the Peacock Angel had become an embodiment of the Serpent was more like a joke than a proper system of belief. It was as if the inversion of all that I held dear had become a testimony to divine obliteration. It seemed that the Yazidis had decided to revoke goodness, and the pursuit of innocence, in order to affirm the right of Satan to existence in his own right.

Such a view must have occurred to the merchant also. When he had concluded his story, he turned to me and made the following confession:

"Good friar," he said. "I came here to seek your advice. It is said that you know more about the ways of the world than any man alive. Is it not so that men come from all points of the compass to share with you their knowledge?"

I confessed to him that this was true. I was at pains to assure him, however, that they mostly met with me in order to convey their perceptions, gleaned as they were from what they had witnessed, rather than to share with me their uncertainties. My own knowledge of the world, I insisted, was derived from theirs entirely.

"The eyes of the mind can often be blinded by the glare of experience," he observed.

I asked him to continue.

"The emir of the Yazidis struck me as a pious man," he went on. "Knowing that he worshiped the Devil made it difficult for me to reconcile myself to the workings of Providence. If the man worships evil rather than goodness—and equally, he respects Our Lord, while we, in contrast, despise the Devil—does this not suggest to you how we have built up a barrier between ourselves and the principle of darkness? The Yazidis, these followers of Satan who have adopted the ritual practices of all creeds, have they not managed to embrace the entire human experience, while we choose to reject the beliefs of others? It is questions like these that I hoped you might be able to answer for me."

The merchant had indeed posed a riddle. All my knowledge of the world had not prepared me to answer such questions; one needed the wisdom of Solomon for that! The mere fact that the Yazidis had survived since Assyrian times intimated to me how practical their accommodation with the Devil had been. Living in league with the Fallen Angel had in some way made them feel that they were wanted by him, or that he needed them. From their point of view, evil was obviously important to the world. Clearly the Yazidis, for all their entanglement with the Serpent, were one of the few people with the courage to believe in the duality of being. By elevating a murderer to sainthood (a gardener, no less: shades of Eden!), they obviously felt the need to nurture rather than disown whatever despair they might feel as a consequence of his act.

"I know their views are anathema to us," the merchant remarked. "But though they have suffered oppression on many occasions, the Yazidis have somehow managed to survive. Does it not say something? They cling to a belief in the Devil because to them he embodies a principle of virtue. I must say that my sojourn at Ba-Idri has given me cause for considerable doubt with regard to my own beliefs. It was as if the sandstorm had deliberately set out to divert our caravan to this remote and somber settlement so my companions and I might confront a set of opposing beliefs that really did appear to work."

The Levantine merchant's confusion was contagious. He had carried this heavy burden around half a world in the hope of receiving some enlightenment. Already my map was beginning to become laden with a mass of conflicting views. The Yazidis and their Devil worship merely added a new dimension to the perplexity of my task. How could I portray in the margin a portrait of Malak Taus, the Peacock Angel, knowing that he represented an all-pervading darkness? I asked this same question of the merchant, hoping that he might be able to help.

"Good friar, it appears that you and I have reached the same conclusion," he said. "For whatever distinction we give to the reality of truth as a measure of the absolute, inevitably we find it destroying the very substance from which it is fashioned."

A smile appeared on the merchant's face as he spoke. He had managed to extract from his own confusion an answer to our mutual quandary. For he had discovered at the heart of the Yazidis' belief in the idea of duality and darkness a new principle of unity. Cleary, what these people believed was that the unity lying in the heart of Our Lord must remain forever dissoluble in ourselves if we are ever to know the difference between good and evil.

14

HE IDEA THAT MEN in foreign climes
might adhere to beliefs contrary to our own,
even as they respected a third, was brought
home to me with considerable force after a
visit by a teacher of rhetoric during his recent visit from
Libya. Familiar with the duplicity of language, he nevertheless informed me how his researches into a lost people
known as the Garamantes had led him to formulate certain conclusions after studying artifacts he had found in
their tombs.

"We know nothing about how they spoke or thought,"
the teacher of rhetoric informed me, while at the same
time offering as a gift a painted ostrich egg that he had
discovered in a Garamantian tomb. "It seems they had no
written language."

I asked him whether this was so unusual, given that the Garamantes had long ago disappeared from the pages of history.

"So too have the Egyptians, yet we we suspect that their beliefs are concealed among the hieroglyphs on their tombs," replied the teacher.

My visitor went on to outline what he had surmised about Garmantian culture. Outside the tombs he had visited among the rocky outcrops of Libya stood altars built in the form of horns or obelisks. Such symbols, he informed me, were striking evidence of the Garamantians' allegiance to not one but *two* systems of belief.

"The horn they obviously borrowed from the Egyptians and their sun god, Horus," he explained, "while the obelisk must have been borrowed from the Carthaginians and their cult of Tanit."

Judging from this evidence, my visitor was of the opinion that the Garamantes had not subscribed to beliefs of their own—or if they had, then they had done so in secret. On the evidence so far gathered, it appeared they were a people who were happy to borrow from others what they themselves lacked. Unable to decide the superiority of one set of beliefs over another, the Garamantes had simply opted for both. In the opinion of my visitor, however, such an approach had contributed to their extinction. They had become victims of others more powerful than themselves (namely, the Romans), who wanted them to adhere to their own religious practices at the expense of

those borrowed from the Egyptians and the Carthaginians.

"In terms of thought and of belief, it appears that the
Garamantians were forced to become a subject race," the
teacher of rhetoric maintained.

His argument was based on a floor mosaic he had wit
nessed in an ancient Roman villa near Zliten. In one of
the pictures he observed a Garamantes youth, probably a
captured warrior, standing erect in an open cart. Tied to
a pole, the young man was already bleeding from wounds
inflicted by a leopard that had been set loose on him as
part of a circus performance. Though dying, the young
Garamantes appeared strikingly impassive to those watching his demise. He wore his affliction as one of the
damned with an air of forbearance, even calm.

"The Garamantes probably suspected they had nothing
to offer that might justify their survival," my visitor argued. "Since it is likely that they worshiped the sun and
wind, and looked to the spirits of place to bestow order
upon their lives, they knew that such beliefs would be
anathema to the Romans. The horn and obelisk found by
their tombs were very likely little more than an elaborate
camouflage placed there to conceal their deep-seated reverence for the natural forces about them. I suspect it was
this extraordinary freedom of belief that so unsettled their
captors, and so made them an object of suspicion. They
were a people bonded to nature more than they were to
the tenets of those who had lost faith in its power."

I asked the teacher of rhetoric whether he genuinely believed the extinction of the Garamantes could be linked to the idea of pagan idols being worshiped and subsequently scorned as a genuine form of religious practice.

"What else can I believe?" he replied, gazing for a long moment at the painted ostrich egg on the table before us. "They were content with their spiritual polygamy before becoming circus fodder to the Romans. In due time, it appears, they found themselves, as you suggest, lost even to the pages of history. They no longer existed as a distinct race. They simply disappeared.

"I am beginning to ask myself whether belief in the sun and wind carries with it a death sentence," he went on in a somber tone. "Is it true that a people who invoke false gods must be condemned to depart this life at the hands of that which they most hold in reverence? On the evidence suggested to us by the mosaic at Zletin, the Garamantes found themselves playing the role of sacrificial victim in a circus designed to affirm their animality rather than their humanity. I am beginning to believe that, in the eyes of those Roman onlookers at least, both leopard and youth were conjoined in an act of mutual destruction. It was as if nature were being asked to destroy itself."

What was I to think? So far my encounter with the teacher of rhetoric from Libya had confirmed certain facts that had already begun to emerge from the process of gathering information for my map. Each encounter with an alien race had furnished me with new insights into the depiction of an imaginary landscape. Recent visitors had reinforced what I had long suspected: that beyond the region of thought with which I was so familiar were certain layers of perception that hitherto I had not experienced.

Plainly the Garamantes were a case in point. From what my visitor had told me about them, they had placed themselves on the same level as other living creatures, other creatures of God, that they might define their place alongside them. Unfortunately this had not appealed to the Romans. They did not like the idea of a people who defied their state-oriented belief in the supremacy of the human. In the end, the leopard had become an instrument of destruction for them rather than an object of reverence, destroying once and for all the delicate relationship the Garamantes had held with the cosmos itself.

"To my way of thinking," my visitor observed, "the Garamantes woke up one morning to find their beliefs rendered impotent by overlords who despised their spiritual independence. Is it not the curse under which we all labor, even today?"

I remarked to the teacher of rhetoric that I considered that my own beliefs, rooted as they were in Our Lord's death and redemption, savored of truth more than most.

"Isn't this precisely my point?" he replied. "The Garamantes revered the wind and rain as the embodiment of their vision of truth also. Now they are lost to the world."

He did have a point. How could I place on my map a memory of a people who had ceased to exist because of a dispute over their beliefs? To do so would be like treading on a field of thorns. Loathe as I was to admit the veracity of his logic, I had to concede that the world—the world I was attempting to realize, anyway—was a lesser place for the Garamantes' nonexistence. In the Libyan hinterland now lying empty on my map, what could I possibly draw in but a certain sameness, even a blandness, since these people have all disappeared from the face of the earth?

"You could describe with your pen and brush what they gave to the world," the teacher insisted. "Whatever one might say, these people have in some way survived their bout with the leopard. The horn and obelisk have not obscured what was most intensely theirs, however much their tombs might be dominated by their presence. I believe your map of the world should include their absence."

I asked my visitor what, exactly, he meant.

"The Garamantes reflect something inside us all," he replied. "That they are no longer with us does not mean we cannot enjoy what was an inherent innocence in their nature. Belief in the sun, wind, and the spirit of place confirms it, does it not? Nor could the Romans erase such a gift from the face of the earth, try as they might. It remains with us, even today. Hence the need for you to render it on your map for others to enjoy."

The teacher of rhetoric had put forward a powerful argument for the retention of such lost knowledge. Meanwhile, I would have to draw upon all my ability as an illustrator if I were to describe a people already lost to the world. I might have to begin by rendering on paper the finely decorated ostrich egg lying on the table. It alone was the sole clue I possessed to indicate who the Garamantes had been prior to their extinction. Had they not enjoyed during their lifetime an uncommon clarity, and perception, in their worship of nature, which had granted them the grace of such freedom? It was hard to tell. What was evident in their behavior even at the end, however, was that only when freedom joined with nature did they realize themselves.

15

OW GOES MY WORLD? Outspread and
undulating it lies on the table, a great orb of
intractable terrain. Zones of pure space extend to the farthest reaches of my imagination. It is a world made up of much more than kingdoms
and continents. It is a realm known only to those who
have an eye to seeing what is invisible, or to those who are
prepared to elevate themselves above the light of understanding.

Such a map intimates the earth's supreme aloneness. By
the light of a candle, coastlines appear to tremble ever so
slightly before my gaze. They pulsate with the movement
of endless unseen tides. Every mountain range is glaciered
with shimmering ice. Travelers to such regions return with
reports that do little justice to the exhilaration they have

felt. Remote mountain tracks disappear in their footsteps, leaving them confined to their solitude more completely than if they had been in prison. Meanwhile their thoughts march ahead in search of a fertile valley, a hospice, a haven. They are forever trudging toward the prospect of knowing more about themselves.

If I had known what blankness would ultimately surround me when I began the task, perhaps I would have chosen to remain behind these walls of secure meditation and not address myself to the discovery of the world. San Michele is, after all, its own small world. I am told that every act of adventure can be realized here within the daily rounds of prayer, ritual, and plainsong. Greater edifices than this monastery have been constructed from the mystic endeavor espoused by such ideals. It is true, sometimes men in harness to grace are more powerful than a whole army whose allegiance is suspect.

My map absorbs me with what it does not reveal. Each time I gaze upon it I am captivated by what so far has not been included within its margins. I am greedy to know more, to discover new countries, peoples, their mores. Who but a humble monk confined by the Rule is better suited to voyage beyond its impositions? I may be constrained by my vows, but even these cannot prevent me from desiring to overcome the limitations I have imposed upon myself.

"The southern zone has a warm climate," wrote the Spanish monk Beatus of Liebana in his commentary on the Apocalypse. "It is unknown to the sons of Adam. It has no links with our race. No human eye has seen it. Access is barred to men, and the sun makes it impossible to enter this region. In the opinion of the philosophers it is inhabited by the Antipodeans, who live through seasons which are the exact opposite to ours."

Is that not how the Antipodians see us? Are we too existing in reverse, upside down, on top of ourselves? I am beginning to wonder whether what I have always believed to be so centered is in fact dispersed. Have I become tired of the known? The more I encounter those who impart to me their knowledge of distance and time, the more I begin to believe that the real object of my quest is to allow myself to become entranced.

What these men bring to me in my study is a feeling of awe. They do not make the trip from Venice simply to relate their interest in the world at large. How many storms have they experienced aboard ships while trying to reach port? Many, if the truth be known. Such men are different from someone like myself. They have made fear their helpmate, their angel, on every occasion when they have ventured forth into the unknown.

Nonetheless, our differences become more manifest whenever I pore over this map. Their knowledge is intrinsic in every gesture that I make. I cannot draw in a coastline, or detail the location of a city, or perhaps mark in an underwater reef without paying lip service to what they have already told me. Every word they have uttered is aided by an accomplice, the darkness of wisdom masquerading as curiosity. These travelers have become the eyes and ears of the world.

If it is so, then what kind of body am I dealing with? Fra Beatus's rather strange maps often look more like a human body, their rivers resembling intestines and veins, their mountains looking like limbs. But we know them to be suspect. They are the maps of a man who saw the world as an extension to the human condition, not as a tree rooted on the edge of an abyss.

There! I have made the same mistake as Fra Beatus. We are both guilty of trying to fix the world with a comparison. For both of us the animality of the letter has become the primary and infinite equivocality that is the sign of the earth.

There is yet more information that I need to glean from my informants if I am to map every part of the world. If it is divided into regions of excessive heat and cold, with two temperate zones between the hot and cold regions, then I need to know more about such conditions before I commit myself to a final version.

To date, my most important visitor has not yet presented himself in my cell. Who is this man whose knowledge will, inevitably, resolve every doubt, every conflict? Is he a man like myself, or will he bear the swarthy complexion of someone who has experienced all the extremities of climate, the scorched and incessant blast of a sun attempting to inhibit his progress?

I gaze at the great empty spaces on my map still awaiting clarification. Their breadth inhibits. And yet I know
these represent the last frontier that I must also cross if I
am to complete my lifelong task.

Grant me strength, O Lord, to venture forth into a region that as yet has not been revealed.

16

 ENICE HAS THE WORLD in the palm of its hand. Every ship that arrives carries in its hold a treasure trove of lies and deceits gathered in distant lands. Merchants in their offices down by the docks are constantly asking for information, so that they might make decisions to their own advantage. More likely than not, they find themselves getting less than they bargained for, in spite of their optimism. Their disappointment, however, only seems to fuel whatever ambition they have to make a profit next time. In the warehouses clerks pore over cargo lists on which almost every item appears to be more substantial than it really is.

Such is the nature of trade. Venetians are masters at creating a demand for what others might not have even heard of. What begins as a quest for an object that at first seems intangible (the horn of a unicorn, for example) usually turns out to have a more prosaic origin (such as that of a whale's tooth). Perhaps it is true of all knowledge: when it is placed in the hands of a craftsman after a long and devious journey from a far country, its patina of mystery is soon scraped away to reveal an object of a more sedate hue.

I mention these things in the light of a book of odes that came into my possession by way of a Venetian trader residing in the Golden Horn at Constantinople. Having heard of my interest in gathering unusual facts about the lands to the east, he sent me the work of an anonymous Persian poet. In his letter the trader informed me that he had been given the work as a gift from an Ottoman merchant with whom he had done business in the past. The long-standing distrust between Europeans and the Grand Turk that continues to exist to this day does not preclude, it appears, the exchange of poetry as a measure of their mutual esteem.

Reading the odes, I was struck by their simplicity. Their metaphors were derived from the earthy splendor of a life lived in a village or on the road. The poet compared love to a coat, the soul to a fountain, affliction to a fire, even a bird to the imagination. All the abstract expressions of thought and feeling that men experience found their counterpart in some image from nature. The poet saw the human condition as a rich field of correspondences that he could draw upon at will.

It turned out that the Persian poet had been inspired by another, a wandering dervish who called no place his home. The dervish had journeyed throughout the Saracen world in search of a man wise enough to answer all his questions. Until he had met the Persian poet, the dervish had begun to believe that his expectations had been ill founded. No man should hope to learn the meaning of life from another: he must seek it elsewhere, under the outspread wings of angels, in sacred groves—even, perhaps, among outcasts. The dervish had set himself a task impossible to realize. Hence his continual wandering, his petulance, his eccentricity and bouts of anger.

Without realizing it, the poet had allowed his sensibility to become so refined, so spiritualized, so absorbed in the business of transcending itself, that his humanity had somehow lost its power to attract others. His solitude was the result of losing contact with the world. He had become immersed in a life without contours, without depth, pain, or indeed normal day-to-day affliction. He had transformed himself into an icon, worshiping his own transformation more than he did the teachings of Allah or those around him.

But the dervish changed all that. His encounter with anguish made him the ideal sounding board for the poet's untried images and metaphors. The dervish believed in the world of ordinary things as a basis for the poet's right to form an image. He insisted that the poet draw his inspiration from this world rather than the next. He wanted him to plunge ever deeper into the turbulent waters of life, that he might surface with a clearer perception of all that is.

According to the dervish, suffering was the only process by which a man might unleash his inner strength. In one of his odes, the poet, drawing upon his awakened insight, likened this process to the tempering of a sword by a blacksmith.

The poet and the dervish became inseparable. They lived together in the same Anatolian hermitage, conversing on topics of interest to them both. Between them, expression and experience were joined in the hope of realizing something tangible. What one lacked, the other was able to provide. Words that previously had proved to be too flighty acquired gravity and so were brought down to earth. In contrast, the dervish's long life of disappointment and frustration was leavened by the poet's intense feelings of joy. The poet refused to allow his friend's bitterness to become the common currency of exchange.

This was why the Venetian trader had received the odes as a gift in the first place. According to the trader's letter, his Ottoman friend had felt the need to use these poems as a medium of exchange. "He told me," the trader wrote, "that the odes reflected the depth of his esteem for me. In spite of the gulf that separates us in terms of our religion and customs he believes that earthy images still have the power to bind us, whether we choose to respect them or not."

It was a startling admission. Two men of opposing beliefs had found a common respect for each other in the odes of another. And the "other" had been made more complete by the intervention of a fourth person, namely, myself. I detected at once a chain of sensibility being forged across the entire world by individuals who had been transformed by a mutual esteem engendered among all of them. It went on and on, this linking of minds and hearts, this creation of a pool of tolerance. In the end Christian and Mohameddan, trader and merchant, poet and dervish, expression and experience, all had contributed to the emergence from the waters of ignorance of an entirely new continent.

Such a continent interested me considerably. At moments of extreme clarity I could see it emerging from the mist of uncertainty that surrounds all great encounters. Of course, I had not expected that its existence might be revealed in the recitation of an ode. All my previous experience had taught me to be wary of the unsubstantiated image, the flight of fancy, any extravagance that might be brought on as a result of a bout of ecstasy. Yet here was a new land being talked about by men who had rarely strayed far from their cargo lists.

All this led me to wonder whether I had been relying too much for my information on substantiated sources.

There can be no doubt that in the past I had been drawn to those reports by travelers who had observed with an unprejudiced eye. Such men had brought back reports that described the world in terms of what they had witnessed, rather than its effect on their souls. In turn, I had translated their information into recognizable coastlines, the very essence of geographic exactitude.

The Venetian trader's letter from Constantinople, together with the inclusion of the Persian odes bestowed upon him by his Ottoman friend, had begun to change all that for me. I now realized that the possibility existed of outlining another form of map altogether. Such a map would include how people experience their country, and how they extract from it a measure of well-being. It would be a map that assumes the role of a testament as much as it situates the earth among the waters.

Needless to say, this map of mine has grown out of all proportion to its size. The four corners of the globe are now filled with an indescribable array of knowledge that previously I would have considered outside its purview. How am I to include a set of odes written by some anonymous Persian poet who happened to befriend a dervish? Is it possible to render affliction as fire, knowing full well that its combustible nature can cause so much damage? I have no wish to see my efforts reduced to cinders.

Surely this is exactly what makes a unicorn's horn so mysterious. While its origin might lie in a whale's tooth, its significance depends upon another consideration altogether, namely, that of interpretation. The map represents none other than the transformation of a whale's tooth into a unicorn's horn. It is not its origin that counts but what it inspires. The craftman's task is to extract a form from what has been given to him, and to make of it something that appeals to the heart as well as the mind.

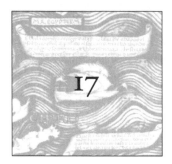

17

N THE ORIENT, I am informed, there exist huge forests populated by exotic animals and flowers. Men who have visited those regions attest to the strange customs of the natives who inhabit them. They speak of striped carnivores known as tigers feeding on victims who go naked but for stripes painted all over their bodies. Some observers maintain that these natives are barely human because of their close association with the animals that eat them, and so are excluded from the fraternity of civilized men.

Such reports from Sumatra, Java, and the Moluccas suggest that verdancy can be contagious. Entire communities live out their lives in the shade of huge leaves, which protect them from seasonal rains. They practice strange rites, some of which involve the eating of human flesh.

The idea that men might eat one another as part of a sacrificial ritual seems like a grave aberration, for I am not prepared to believe that the consumption of one unfortunate victim may lead to the renewal of another. In no other way, however, can I account for what otherwise might be considered a normal practice among animals.

On other maps I have studied, by such men as Gerardus Mercator and Abraham Ortelius, there is some evidence for the existence of a Great South Land located in the vicinity of Beach and Lochac. Such a land encloses the Antarctic and is in turn joined to Terra del Fuego in the Americas. The region is said to be inhabited by a mysterious race of men who hop about on one huge foot the size of an umbrella, whereupon they use this same foot to shade themselves during the full heat of midday. I can only conclude that there are many wonders yet to discover before any definitive map can be drawn up to account for all the regions of the world.

Take, for example, a visit I received from a Jesuit priest who had recently returned from the Indies. Fra Campeggio, an indefatigable traveler, had been inspired by Marco Polo's journey to Tartary and beyond. With the blessing of the Pope he had gone out to convert the heathen wherever he could. Over the years he had opened missions in India and Malaya, before setting sail for Borneo. Reports had filtered through to him of a jungle people who in the past had spurned Christian and Mohameddan zealots alike. According to Fra Campeggio, these people sought solace from birds rather than any deity on high.

"I took ship on a local Chinese craft," he recounted, "and met up with the bird people shortly after my arrival in Borneo. I had half expected to be confronted with men wearing feathers! Such were the reports of the tribesmen that I was prepared for almost anything. Instead I found men whose fate was determined by the call of seven sacred birds."*

Fra Campeggio outlined to me how their religion worked. Seven species of birds had been enlisted in the cause of augury, which formed the basis of their belief. Each time a certain bird uttered its call, this indicated to the listener what might later occur. A more elaborate synthesis would be arrived at, depending on whether the bird call was heard on the right hand or the left, whether it came from ahead or behind, or whether there occurred more than one call at any given time. This collaboration between men and birds extended to the level of a partnership. Nothing was ever done by the villager without consulting the birds and so receiving their permission to engage in any activity they wished.

"The birds had been accorded the status of gods," Fra

---

*The bird men could be the ancestors of the Iban or Sea Dayaks of Borneo, whose dialogue with the birds still goes on today. Sadly, uncontrolled logging of their forests is threatening the habitat of these birds of augury. It is likely that within a decade all converse with the future may be lost.

Campeggio said. "A farmer cannot plant his crops, nor a man take a wife, nor an evil spirit be despatched from a village without the help of these birds. Their trill remains supreme, the pronouncement of a sibyl."

When I asked the good friar whether the people ever ate one another, he shook his head.

"They cherish the heads of their enemies, but it seems the birds will not allow them to eat themselves. Cannibalism is not on their menu," he replied with a smile.

I sighed with relief. Fra Campeggio, whose height must have inspired awe even among Borneo headhunters, was certainly not the type of man to lose his head when confronted by difficult circumstances. He was a man whose certitude was his armor.

"I made a journey into the hinterland with a member of the tribe in order to ascertain for myself whether his power of augury matched that of his explanation," he went on.

"Each bird that we encountered sang to us with a particular plenitude," Fra Campeggio added. "I gained the impression that we were in the presence of—let me say— our conscience. There's no other word for it. How on earth can one describe the lofty tone of admonition, or the raucous cry of warning, or perhaps the clear note of joy that came from the throats of such birds? It was as if for the first time I had heard the voice of Nature. Her words, though indecipherable from my point of view, nonetheless pointed to the possibility of entering into a dialogue. My guide, the elderly headhunter, was at pains to translate everything that the birds said. He held nothing back from me."

Fra Campeggio's story was a strange tale indeed, so startling was its implication. Here was a man who had gone out to convert the heathen, who instead had found himself subjected to what might only be called the "language of the birds." Is it any wonder that he did not lose his head under the pressure of such a revelation? Finding himself standing under a forest canopy in the company of a headhunter, while at the same time listening to the call of seven unseen birds, must have suggested to him that they were responding to a voice from elsewhere. It was a question I asked of the tall Jesuit as he gazed out the window at the cupolas and towers of Venice, glowing in the afternoon light, across the water.

"All my experience and knowledge could not teach me how to respond," he agreed. "Remember, I was in the presence of a man who had tried and then rejected cannibalism in favor of possessing another man's head as a part of his custom. What was I to say? We did not share the same world. His guides were birds, while mine were the injunctions of Our Lord. Does not this signify the difference between us? Though both of us, I suppose, were grappling with the same inner voice masquerading in outwardly different forms."

Fra Campeggio had obviously thought a good deal about his experience in the Borneo jungle during his homeward voyage. Who wouldn't? He had journeyed to the end of the earth to convert a people he had never met before. In this respect he had been unsuccessful: he admitted to me that while he was among them no head-hunters ever abandoned their beliefs in favor of his own.

But he did make an interesting observation: "While with the augurer, I was reminded of the words of the great Irish cleric Columbanus.* He maintained that those who wished to know the lofty profundity of things need to study Nature first. To comprehend the deep sea of under-standing, it is important to observe the sea itself. If you wish to understand the Creator, then understand the crea-ture. I suspect that this is what the headhunter was trying to show me. His interest in the birds, however odd it ap-peared to me at first, was in some way evidence of Colum-banus's entreaty. He was trying to tell me that the symbol was closer to the essential nature of the invisible than its interpretation."

To think that the Borneo headhunter had succeeded in matching wits with a learned Jesuit! It did not seem possi-ble. In the presence of Fra Campeggio, seven mysterious birds had somehow orchestrated a significant doctrine that accorded created things the role of revealing what is nor-

---

*Saint Columban was a sixth-century Irish monk noted for his abstemious character and penchant for the seclusion offered by the hos-tile forests of Gaul. He transmuted pilgrim fervor into an existential theology in a series of sermons or *instructiones,* which have been col-lected and edited by G. S. M. Walker as *Sancti Columbani Opera* (Dublin, 1970).

mally accessible only to the intellect. These remote bird men of the jungle had managed to put into practice a doctrine that my confreres and I still have not completely resolved.

One question remained: How did these savage men arrive at such subtle conclusions when they were victims of an insatiable desire to possess other men's heads? I could not equate such behavior with my own understanding of what the head was meant to represent. As the seat of the intellect, it was hard to imagine it being reduced to a mere decoration outside a hut. Yet according to Fra Campeggio, that is exactly what these bird men of the Borneo jungle preferred.

"I suspect they had confused the imagination with the intellect," Fra Campeggio observed. "The calls of birds had become a clarion, drawing them away from the savagery of their customs but only for a brief moment. The fact remains that collecting human heads preoccupied them. They had not yet learned to recognize the similarity between what they created in their own minds as a result of a bird's call, and what they sought to remove from another man when they decapitated him.

"The imaginative faculty, when not joined to the intellect, is a flighty thing, as we all know. But it's also precious. If you treat it as a mere object, then how easy it is to destroy. By worshiping birds these tribesmen were able to preserve the power of imagination within themselves. When they chose to decapitate their enemies, they were wrenching it from another. This is why they found it impossible to embrace the teachings that I offered them. The language of the birds, so to speak, did not extend to communicating to them how powerful the intellect can be in its own right."

I asked the learned Jesuit whether the birds had provided him with insight into his own fate while he was among them.

"How can I be certain?" he replied. "While my guide was at pains to translate each call, his interpretation lacked the formal clarity I was hoping to hear. Each trill, you see, could be interpreted in different ways. I was left with the task of discerning Nature's message for myself."

I suggested to him that such an explanation might concur with the views of Columbanus.

"The book of Nature is written in many languages," Fra Campeggio admitted. "Not the least that of the birds. My only wish is that headhunting will one day be eliminated from the customs of the bird men. When it happens, they will have finally dispensed with the need to possess the physicality of the mind, and instead will look to its interpretive powers as an extension of the intellect. In this way their imaginative faculty will be matched by something far more lofty."

18

IS VISIT TO THE JUNGLE of Borneo was not the only story Fra Campeggio related to me during the course of our discussions. While waiting to take ship in various Oriental ports, he was able to learn more about the legendary South Land of Lochac that I mentioned earlier. Sailors and Macassan fishermen, some of whom had ventured ashore on its wild and inhospitable coast, spoke of it as a place where no civilized being could survive. If it was not inhabited by one-footed men, then other stories suggested that a race of dark people lived there who embraced nudity as a substitute for clothing.

"I met a Dutch sailor who had been shipwrecked there," Fra Campeggio explained. "As one of the few survivors of a storm, he was forced to resort to cannibalism to appease his hunger. He told me that had he known the aftereffect of such behavior, he would have far preferred to die. The taste of his shipmates remains in his mouth to this day, and he cannot erase it, as much as he has tried. Although he informed me that men tasted like pork, it did not help. Their limbs continued to accost him, even in his dreams. Arms, legs, torsos—all of them rose up to torment him. Half mad, and but skin and bone when I met him, he deeply repented his actions.

"His contact with the natives of Lochac made him reconsider his attitude toward nudity," he added. "Daily seeing their bodies encouraged him to view them more as a visual pleasure, rather than as the meal he might have considered them to be in the past. He discovered that the natives used their bodies as veritable spirit maps on which they used to draw the place where they had been conceived. These people expressed the land in which they lived as symbols daubed all over their bodies."

Fra Campeggio's remarks caught me by surprise. The idea of a body map had not occurred to me before. Rather than carrying about with them an elaborate piece of parchment detailing the earth's contours and coastlines, the natives had chosen to use their own bodies to express what they had discovered about their homeland. They had made their bodies a projection of their world.

"Correct," Fra Campeggio encouraged my ruminations. "What we clothe and keep secret by force of habit, the people of Lochac choose to integrate with their place of abode. According to the Dutchman, who remained with them for some years, each native torso became the embodiment of a sacred landscape. In his eyes it had been transformed from a meal to a missal. What the signs and symbols on the men's bodies represented was the knowledge they had gleaned from their own earth. Such knowledge was much older than the individual concerned: it had been acquired over many generations and constituted what we consider to be customary lore."

Was he suggesting that the human body had become for the people of Lochac a haven of values over and above its organs? Tentatively I put this question to Fra Campeggio, realizing as I did so the paradoxical nature of any conclusion that he might be able to offer.

"That's one way of looking at it, yes," the tall Jesuit replied. "What we consider to be our physical entity, often a sinful one at that, the natives regarded as a living testimony. Their bodies had become a palimsest on which the entire world could be transcribed and then removed in accordance with a ritual process. You can imagine how all this affected the Dutchman. Whereas he had earlier taken to looking at the body as a source of food, he soon learned that its physicality was not its main attribute. As far as the natives were concerned, their bodies were a rich source of knowledge. In contrast to the Dutchman's view, its physicality had become a mere adjunct to what was its primary purpose of representing their world in miniature."

I was astounded by his remarks. The learned Jesuit had introduced me to an entirely new perception of mapmaking. Not only had he journeyed widely in his search for such information (on the pretext of converting others), but he had also managed to bring back an idea I had never conceived of before: that nudity is its own world. It possesses its own climate of beauty, its own meridian of sanctity. The nude body is our primary presence, the first land we encounter when we enter the world. No wonder the poor Dutchman felt that he had betrayed himself when he embarked upon his brief but unhappy career as a cannibal. He had been forced to eat what the natives of Lochac had considered to be the sacred realm of themselves.

"As you can readily imagine, the Dutchman's tale struck me with considerable force," Fra Campeggio continued. "His demeanor, though verging on that of a madman, made me realize how important it is to take leave of oneself on occasion if one is to come to terms with what one inhabits. The body is more than a physical terrain. It has its symbolic value also. Though of course one recognizes that the Dutchman's actions of eating others is reprehensible, one should also remember how we too consume ourselves in our insatiable desire to overcome mortality.

"On the other hand, it seems that the natives of Lochac view the body in a way different from ours. For them, the body partakes of the eternal each time they daub it with the country of their conception. The whole earth is implanted on their bodies whenever they enter into a ritual relation with it.

"For my part," the learned Jesuit concluded, "I realized the futility of my endeavors. How was I to journey to such a place in order to convert them? Impossible! The Dutchman had done me a great favor if he had but known. His heathenish behavior had taught me an important lesson. I could no longer teach people to spurn the body when I knew that it had helped him to survive. Furthermore, he had been fortunate enough to experience its sublime value through the eyes of others."

Fra Campeggio fell silent. In my cell the air did not move. Everything was still, including the movement of our thoughts. We had journeyed so far together and encountered so many strange things, that I asked myself whether I would ever know enough to complete what I had started. The inhospitable coastlines that I had so far transcribed on my map may better be transferred to that region nearer my heart. There, perhaps, they might intimate a continent of indescribable glory, a place that still retains vestiges of that legendary Golden Age so popular among poets and storytellers.

NE MORNING I RECEIVED an unusual missive in the form of a scroll brought to me by a messenger from the East. He was of Oriental appearance and insisted that he had come on the request of his master. When I asked him who his master might be, the messenger replied that he was in the employ of Sun Ssu-mo, a sage at the court of the Chinese emperor. He also informed me that his master, hearing of my work, wished to enter into a correspondence with me on the true nature of the world.

When I replied that my interest lay in charting the outline of the known world rather than entering into a discussion about its substance, the messenger remained unmoved. He told me that his master understood the nature of my research and wanted to contribute what he considered to be important information about the elixirs that make up this world. I was both confused and a little unsettled by this sort of talk, since it implied that the world could be manufactured at will.

"My master has requested I translate his letter to you, so that you might be better informed," the messenger announced with a small flourish of his hand.

The man carefully unrolled the scroll in front of him and began to read Sun Ssu-mo's text:

"It has come to my attention that you, Fra Mauro, a monk of San Michele in the Serene Republic of Venice, have been attempting to create a definitive map of the world. It is a most interesting and worthwhile enterprise—one that is, I believe, fraught with all the uncertainties that accompany any intellectual endeavor. I must commend you.

"I wish to bring to your attention, however, certain discoveries of my own—discoveries that may help you to amend your map to the advantage of us all. Since I have read in succession the lore books of old, I am able to inform you that, beyond doubt, there have been cases of men who sprouted wings and rose effortlessly in flight. This was as a result of taking certain elixirs, of which I will later elaborate.

"I must say," the messenger continued, pausing to analyze the exact meaning of his master's next remark, "I am unable to speak of these things without a feeling of ardent longing in my heart. My sole regret is that this divine Way is remote from most men, its pathway through the clouds so inaccessible. For my part, I have gazed in vain at this azure heaven, not knowing how to ascend to it.

"For many years now I have practiced the technique of preparing such elixirs by cyclical transformations and fixing substances in fire. In this way I have been able to determine the formula for potable jade and liquid gold. By their very nature these elixirs are difficult to fathom and unpredictable.

"In spite of great difficulties I have been able to make considerable progress in this most supreme art. The Nine-fold Radiance and Seven Luminary elixirs are within my grasp. I have labored long and hard, all the while ceaselessly investigating, hoping to discover for myself this special knowledge.

"Thankfully, my wishes have not been frustrated, nor has my determination been broken by these excessive labors. How could I expect a quick and easy recompense for my hard work? The Way of Heaven is impartial, as you know, and I have been forced to wait. Finally I have been rewarded by the discovery of several important formulas, each of which yields not the slightest discrepancy when subjected to normal transformative processes."

The messenger paused for a short while, that I might contemplate Sun Ssu-mo's remarks. I must confess that his line of inquiry was foreign to my ears. What was the man talking about? Had he taken leave of his senses? His views appeared to have nothing to do with cartography, or indeed with anything remotely to do with my work. Sun Ssu-mo had misinterpreted the true nature of my endeavors, and now we were at cross-purposes. The question was whether I might be able to respond in a way that would do justice to the considerable effort he had gone to ensure that I might receive his missive.

"Now, because of man's aspiration being what it is," the messenger resumed, "he values above all his physical existence. But this, as we know, is as evanescent as the dew in spring, perishing as easily as the frost of autumn. It seems that everything passes in the flicker of an eye. Magnificence and penury do not endure for long, nor do melancholy and jubilation last much longer. How sad it is for me to speak of such things!

"I wish to offer you the fruit of my labor. The meaning of the formula I have enclosed will become patent in the text. Since I deem you a friend and a fellow student of the Way, I believe it is important that we share what we know. Should we not? Herein you will find the formula for white jade.

"Take two large clamshells," the messenger continued, slowly reading the formula at the foot of the scroll. "Pulverize and grind them into a fine powder. Put one *chin* of this powder in a bamboo tube, insert some Epsom salts, and seal the ends of the tube tightly. Immerse the tube in fortified vinegar. After twenty days the powdered shells will have liquified. Take one *chin* of quartz, pulverize it, and pour the powder into the tube. Immediately the concoction will coagulate. Extract the product and heat it to redness over a good charcoal fire. Soon it will become white jade, which may be taken internally.

"This," the messenger concluded, "will help you to grow wings."

Grow wings? Why should I wish to do such a thing? The Chinese sage and I were operating on two entirely different levels. While I wished to augment the true dimensions of the world, he was keen to rise above it. White jade or no white jade, however, I had no wish to grow feathers and fly.

"Treat the formula for white jade as meaning something altogether different," the messenger informed me as he carefully rolled up the scroll. "It is not meant to be regarded as an actual event, as something real. My master wishes you to understand that his elixir is, so to speak, an imaginative draft, and should be drunk only at that moment when one desires to attain to a higher awareness. It can happen only when one has decided to abandon one's normal perceptions of the world in order to attain to a deeper sensibility. My master believes that such an eventuality will evoke its own disposition toward flight. Otherwise, how is one ever to rise above oneself?"

How indeed! Sun Ssu-mo must have known of my fear of heights. Yet withall I understood one thing clearly: the elixir for white jade must somehow be incorporated onto my map, even if it were no more than an imaginative draft.

Later, when the messenger had departed, I asked myself why it was that my informants of late had been at pains to advise me of matters not of this world. Were they trying to tell me that my obsession with its physical aspects had in some way restricted the fluency of my research? Was I limiting myself? Evidently some people thought so, otherwise they would not have felt the need to communicate with me in the first place.

Sun Ssu-mo, like his predecessors, must have desired to bring to my attention certain knowledge before it was too late. Without this knowledge in my possession, he probably felt my map would convey a distorted impression of the world's true shape. In the interest of wayfarers of the future, he obviously wanted to be sure that such men did not become lost, owing to the receipt of information whose absolute value was plainly defective. He wanted them to know that the world could also be contrived as an invisible event as potent as the elixir of white jade. Only then, it seems, would men learn how to fly and so transcend its limits.

20

N ORDER TO COMPLETE an exact map of the world, I must learn to look at the problem from another perspective. Instead of trying to define each continent in a way that fixes its reality so that all might agree with my interpretation, I need to be more circumspect in my assertions.

Each of us has the right to speak of his coastline, his mountains, his deserts, none of which conforms to those of another. Individually we are obligated to make a map of our own homeland, our own field or meadow. We carry engraved in our hearts the map of the world as we know it.

Then we begin to cover the world with impressions that we have lived. Such dazzling splendor! These impressions are capable of rising above all the premises of sensibility that we believe are ours. They remain forever free, since we can never enclose their fate in our own. The map we draw becomes a representation of these impressions, each one contributing to that sublime image we believe exists but so far have not yet discovered.

How things are in the world is a matter of complete indifference to someone who measures what he sees according to things fashioned outside it. Perhaps I have been too ready to address the problem in relation to information derived from what we encounter with our senses only. Inadvertently, I have contributed to the creation of my own illusion. I believed that the thoughts and impressions of all my visitors were derived from a certain actuality, at all times palpable, when in truth their remarks had quite obviously passed through the filter of their own sensibility.

What that belief really means is that my map is a distortion. All its representation of terrain and oceans is but the revelation of how I regarded my visitors' perceptions in the first place. I now realize that the world is not real save in the way each of us impresses upon it his own sensibility. More importantly, this sensibility results from a belief in the world being a measurable whole, rather than something that extends beyond time and place.

Yet I am grateful to those who have provided me with the benefit of their illusions. They have journeyed to Venice, to this monastery, from so many distant places in order to share with me the purest of all deceptions—that of their own willingness to be entranced. In the process they have provided me with much to think about. For each man, whether he wandered in the desert or tramped through the jungle, was able to change the nature of space for himself. In so doing, he was able to offer me something important—that wherever one might happen to be, in whatever circumstances, it is impossible to seal off the spirit from its place of growth. The world and the spirit are somehow conjoined. They both thrive on one another as a seed does in the earth.

Who but someone who has quit home and journeyed to distant lands would understand? It has taken me a lifetime to realize that my sedentary nature has provided me with an avenue of escape. I have been too willing to remain where I am rather than take leave of this place and journey to where I am not. I have allowed myself to become constrained.

In contrast, my visitors welcome what they derive from encountering unknown lands. It is only then that their imagination becomes engaged. They take leave of themselves and become different people. They are no longer restricted by the person that is themselves. The unknown world that they have ventured into tastes of an exoticism inherent in their character. What strikes them as so different marks them forever, causing them to carry about in their hearts a vision of repose. They now know that it is impossible to find elsewhere a place consistent with their own inner world.

I am beginning to wonder whether this whole enterprise has been worthwhile. When I began this map I was intent on realizing a certainty, and now the reverse has proved to be true. No continent or people have turned out to exist except in relation to themselves. Their geographic location has also proved to be deceptive. The inescapable conclusion is that the true location of the world, of its countries, mountains, rivers, and cities, happens to lie in the eye of the beholder. Only there does its individual features partake of that dream quality that one associates with invention.

"The world is like a luminous wheel," an astronomer from distant Eran-Vej wrote to me one day, hearing of my quest and wanting to contribute to it in some way, "where each country is but one spoke among many. It turns upon itself, lighting up the space in which it moves. We are blinded by its transitions."

The astronomer had perceived the earth's movement in relation to the heavens. He had looked beyond the world in order to comprehend its dimension. Further, he had identified something extremely significant, one that I had not considered before: that the earth has a center, and in turn is governed by an immovable point located somewhere beyond, in the universe.

"The world you are looking for," the astronomer expounded, "includes many things whose existence most people doubt. That is because they are expecting those things to conform to what they already know. The world I am talking about has been created to reflect each person's deepest image of himself. It follows that wise men contemplate the world, knowing full well that they are contemplating themselves."

The astronomer had made his point, if not directly, then at least with a certain grave subtlety. What he meant was that the normal process of thinking was not capable of dealing with the world as it is. Such a world emerges not from the sea as an island appears to do after a long voyage, but from a state of enchantment inspired by the mind taking leave of itself. It becomes a place of annihilations, abysses, and epiphanies that have been fashioned during that intermediate state between waking and sleeping, when the senses are still asleep.

"For example," the astronomer continued, "some men living in this region believe that each person views the earth in accordance with his capacity. He cannot see it otherwise. His perception is like glass, which, as we know, is made from a mixture of silica and potash. These ingredients are dense and opaque, and are transformed into the clarity that we recognize as being the substance of glass only by the introduction of heat. In this way the dross is removed. Fine glass is made as a result of careful attention to the process of fusion. According to the sages living in the region, our own vision of the earth is fashioned in much the same way. It, too, can be made as transparent as fine glass, provided the right means are used. The reverse may also occur if certain impurities of thought are not eradicated."

Strange as it may seem, I understood what he meant. The astronomer had resorted to an unusual allusion to explain the kind of world he envisioned. He was trying to tell me that all we picture to ourselves or see with our eyes is inseparable from ourselves. Such things do not exist except as an extention of that inner world to which we give so little credence in the conduct of our normal daily lives.

21

AM READY. My nibs have been sharpened, and all the parchment that I require is at hand. My inks have been carefully mixed. I have prayed to Our Lord also, asking Him to guide my deliberations at every turn. This final rendition of my map, made from previous sketches, must affirm the existence of the world I have discovered with as much honesty as I can muster.

Once again I draw in the margins, complete with cherub-faced winds, arabesques, and small tribal cameos. Other decorations feature mermaids and dragons, together with a variety of strange animals. My name I append to a statement of my intent as a cartographer, while across the top of the page I inscribe a suitable title: *Orbis*

Terrae Compendiosa Descriptio. There. I have announced my intention. My world is about to be realized.

For a moment my thoughts are filled with all the impressions that have been granted to me by others. The journals, the letters, the long conversations with visitors to my cell, the late nights copying up what I have heard, all these drift back to me like so many leaves eddying along a path. Each turn of phrase is saturated with what was once unforeseeable. These observations are now mine. It is as if I am apprenticed to their sense of freedom at last.

But it is hard to begin. How is one to inscribe so much that is invisible to the eye? All my work has become a gesture of trust. Everything I now know is based on the perspective of others. It is as if they, not I, are responsible for the movement of my nib. They control the limits that I am straining to reach. Beyond these, I am entering a no-man's-land, guided only by a belief in the ultimate value of what I am doing.

Careful now, I keep saying to myself. One slip of the nib, one small error in the act of copying, and I will have allowed a distortion to creep into the map. Such an error, however insignificant, will become the hallmark by which my work will be judged by future generations. I will be seen as someone who has introduced a lie into my realization of the world.

Yet, strangely, I have everything and nothing to gain. Our Lord's injunction about gaining the whole world at the cost of one's soul is most appropriate. The world I wish to realize is intimately linked to the possibility of such a loss. I know in my heart, in the deepest recesses of my person, the map that is about to unfold before me will lay out once and for all the extent of my world. Nor can this be torn from me save at the point of death, which stalks me even as I attempt to take possession of the world in all its timelessness.

The coastlines of Africa, India, and portions of the Americas begin to unravel like thread on the parchment. My eye travels down these, calling in at ports where I exchange merchandise in accordance with my whim. I take aboard silk, spices, rare gems, inlaid scimitars, ointments made from the horns of animals, rare books, figurines, pharaonic texts, shrunken heads, slaves, philters, alchemical retorts, tapestries and carpets, leopards in cages, parrots, peacock's feathers, jewelry, pottery, ingots of gold and silver, amber beads and aphrodisiacs, so much that the world hankers for from those distant shores. The cargo I carry in my mind is of such richness that no wealth could possibly be offered in exchange.

Mountains rise from these continents. Snow glistens on the high slopes, its whiteness absorbing the winter sun. Rivers flow toward the sea. Nomads wander plains, their herds grazing on small pockets of grasslands after rains. Great trees are there, filled with orchids, monkeys, and pythons. Bird calls too, the deep trill of invisibility calling to its mate. Huts built of bamboo appear in clearings, smoke seeping through their thatch. Children play in cataracts while fish jump in fright.

I notice men performing rituals, their bodies bare of clothing, their chests daubed in ocher. A pig is trussed to a pole, awaiting sacrifice. Men are pounding drums, and dancers are beating out a rhythm with their feet. Skulls are lined along racks at the entrance to meetinghouses, some of them with shells fixed by resin into their eye sockets. Gaudy feathers are attached to headdresses, and masks imitate the countenance of spirits. Young women are performing love rites, their lithe bodies oiled and sensuous. Older men stand in groups leaning on their spears. A wild animal roars in the thicket, and antelope leap to safety with all the agility of butterflies.

I see houses built of mud standing in clusters on the edge of a desert, waterwheels being slowly turned by camels wearing blindfolds. There are temples filled with many-armed statues, flower-draped altars, food offerings on stone floors. I hear orchestras of musicians sitting cross-legged by temple gates. Female dancers perform a story with the aid of expressive fingers and eyes. Gold-studded clothing glints with the movement of their bodies.

Caravans snake their way among sand dunes watched over by bandits. Inns and caravanseries are filled with travelers. Pilgrims sleep near wayside shrines or by wells reputed to have medicinal qualities. Old men sit on carpets outside their tents reading from texts lying open on wooden stands. Small market towns are bulging with produce, farm animals, and acrobats. Fortune tellers observe the peregrinations of pigeons on a grid chalked in the square. A man charms a snake with his flute.

Armies are on the march, great companies of janissaries, horsemen, cannoniers, archers, and swordsmen. Wherever one looks there are villages in flames, cities under siege, towers crumbling under the weight of constant bombardment. Valiant men stand on parapets trying to ward off scaling ladders. Cauldrons of oil simmer on fires along the entire length of smoking ramparts. The wounded lie in hospitals attended by nurses who serve them food on silver plate. The smell of gunpowder and burnt lint permeates bastions. Everywhere death hovers.

Sages preach in mosques, under acacia trees, in chapels. They mortify themselves on beds of nails, with whips, through acts of abstinence, and by withdrawing into the wilderness. Men meditate over texts handed down to them from avatars. Pilgrims gather about them to hear their message, and their words are passed around like manna, relieving these people of their hunger. Saints abjure their flock to follow the straight way on pain of losing their souls. Everywhere the message is the same, for men are eager to draw strength from the experience of others.

Ships ply sea lanes, their sails billowing with the energy of the wind. Storms threaten, as do the ships of foreign navies. Across the world men pit themselves against the elements, and against others too, in their quest for a measure of well-being. Not a day goes by that a man does not consider what he must do in order to secure a living. Work is his mainstay. With effort he is able to survive.

Monks paint portraits of Our Lord, the saints, and Our Lady in hilltop monasteries. In far-off America prisoners are put to death to appease the sun god. Ceramicists in Anatolian villages visualize abstractions on tiles. Weavers in India hang their looms in trees in the cool of the afternoon. Fountains splash in silent courtyards. Praise singers utter epithets in honor of their lords, while in deep ravines women gather to pound clothes clean on rocks.

Men argue in public places. Women gossip in closed rooms. Potentates give orders and sentence men to death with the merest movement of the hand. Young lovers hurry to their trysting place behind bushes where they taste passion for the first time. Fathers curse their lost honor when the marriage vigils of their daughters reveal no virginal blood at dawn. Women pen letters to their lovers, knowing that they will never see them again. And in the prostitutes' quarter, men slip indoors into the arms of those who have placed a price on the value of their charms.

Doctors, lawyers, clerks, coachmen, sailors, cobblers, blacksmiths, seamsters, builders, footmen, armorers, gunsmiths, painters, architects, sculptors, mapmakers, boatbuilders, notaries, farmers, husbandmen, beekeepers, servants, cooks, glassblowers, oarsmen, elephant handlers, cameleers, fishermen, soothsayers, prophets, surgeons, hunters, millers, apothecaries, officers, saddlers, pilots, laborers, merchants, jewelers, weavers, milliners, wig makers, butchers, augurs, bards, dressmakers, workers in leather, shepherds, vintners, rope makers, storytellers, musicians, carpenters, actors, priests, undertakers, these and many others begin to populate the country I have drawn. Each discipline figures large in the city that I envision.

The map is starting to take on an unusually extravagant shape. Yet so much of what I know has not been drawn in any recognizable way. Is it because the limits of my language restrict the kind of world I want to create? Perhaps, too, I am a victim of an insatiable desire to reason, yet equally I want to place on my map more than logic will allow. I am beginning to accept that what makes the world what it is has its origin elsewhere.

Does that mean that everything is as it is because of this inexplicable origin, this infallible beginning lying everywhere and nowhere at the same time? If it were so, then it follows that no absolute value can exist save that which lies outside this world. Otherwise, would it not become yet another mysterious relativity like ourselves, condemned as we are to old age and death? If it were so, then it would be as fragmentary and as disjointed as all else that exists within this world.

O God! How can this be? Immortality rejects all that I am thinking in the name of absolutes. And yet . . .

T LAST I HAVE COMPOSED the world. The monk in me has attempted to go to the very heart of things. I have sliced through its materiality. I have peeled back its corporeal skin to reveal its inner workings. No man has worked more sincerely than I to render up its inner harmony.

Mapping its surface has placed me in the invidious position of a martyr, it seems. I sought freedom in its unabashed spaciousness and found death instead. For in the act of sharing their knowledge, certain men gave up a portion of their lives to me. Added together, their several losses amount to a death that is my own, since I have taken upon myself what they have chosen to give up.

Gazing at the map, I begin to see a portrait of myself. All the diversity of the world is intimated on the parchment, even as this diversity is intimated within me. An aura of remoteness hovers about its contours, as it does about my head, clarifying what I see. Both the map and myself cling to the invisibility of what we represent. Nor is the tension between us that of myself and it, but of the merging of these. The map and myself are the same.

What am I to do with this document? Should I offer it to the fraternity of voyagers who have made the world their own—the explorers, pilgrims, and merchants who know no limits to their travels? Would they recognize familiar territory among its rhumb lines and wind roses? Or would they dismiss its immateriality as the gropings of a mountebank? It is hard to know how others might judge this map made up of the dreams and visions of one man— no, of a host of men who have charged it with their significance.

I am at a loss to know what to do with it. My *mappa mundi* lies on my desk, a piece of incandescence, a visionary recital. There is no place for it to reside, anywhere, except in the hearts of men, among their most secret thoughts. I begin to liken it to a heavenly event. No matter what people might say, I have emptied matter of its content. Now it shimmers, diaphanous, a subtle body whose origin lies elsewhere.

Have these vain and persistent interrogations brought me any closer to understanding the true nature of the world? All its multiplicity has given rise to a certain wonder; this much I will admit. Yet I am left with a sense of existing in an unfathomable void, surrounded by blankness, as if my desire to come to terms with it has proved fruitless. While its forms, though sensory, have suggested so much more, I have come to believe that consciousness itself is at stake—and too, that a hidden pleroma of intelligence is at work that refuses to reveal its methods.

How do I extract myself from such a quandary? I might throw myself at the feet of these forms and cry out for mercy. On the other hand, I might take courage and plunge into their oceanic possibility, acknowledging them as integers of something more sublime. Who knows how I will resolve the problem? The world awaits my intervention, not as an overlord, but as a cohort. For too long I have allowed myself to remain wrapped in isolation, in the monastic calm of my habitude. I have not had the courage to venture forth into a world that thrives on community, on interdependence and conflict, on the real earth of existence.

I cannot leave the world. All my monads are derived from it, and to it they must return. The conspiracy of escape that has surrounded me for so long has left me with the illusion that I can leave, if not in body, then at least as something else. How misguided I have been all these years! My body and my soul are inseparable. They carry the same weight of finitude even as I struggle to shrug it off. What I have to do is accept this burden, this battle with cessation, for the consummate gift that it is, and live, knowing that death is life's polarity, the feather placed upon the opposing tray to ensure that all is balanced.

I now know that the visitor I have been expecting all these years, the one in whom I have placed so much faith in providing me with the answers I so fervently sought, is none other than myself. I am my own informant, the only person capable of expressing the innate knowledge that resides in all of us. In me lies all the knowledge of the world, since it is my world alone that I wish to explore.

For years I have watched men come ashore, dressed in a cape and sometimes equipped with a sword, hoping that they might be the embodiment of me, the one person I truly know and understand. But they were not me. They were themselves. I deluded myself into believing that I lived a different life independent of myself. This has been my folly to think that my world might be duplicated in another.

There is not much more to do. My map is a masterpiece, even if I do say so. I am well satisfied. With the help of others I have completed the world. It now has a form that is both physical and—dare I say it?—immaterial at once. Perhaps, yes, even mystical. Though there is much left to discover about it in years to come, my small contribution will remain a mark of my own achievement. Humility is not at issue here. I am talking about the exhilaration I feel knowing just how far a man can go in affirming his existence in relation to his peers. May the world I have fashioned be but a first step in the creation of many others as rich as this one!

Yet my strength appears to be failing. It seems strange, but I can barely hold up my nib. The candle at my elbow wavers. A strange lethargy appears to have taken hold of me, causing me to feel weak yet exhilarated at the same time. I do not know why, or whence it has come. It is not high summer, and we are too far from the marshes on the mainland to be influenced by their infectious airs. This lassitude is overpowering. It is as if I am partly suspended in the room, as if those objects about me have no real body. What is happening? All I want to do is fall asleep. Yet I can't: before me lies the summation of my life. This map of the world, for all its flaws, is as scintillant as a rapier in sunlight.

Even at this moment I know that something within me is beginning to shift. I am sailing at last, as if absorbed into the margins of my map, a ship embarking upon its maiden voyage. I am traveling toward a supreme uncertainty, or have inadvertently become a part of some endless continental drift. Who but those who have made a journey beyond this world will understand what I mean? All I know is that for me at least, freedom is at last restored. The realization that I am traveling nowhere in particular has given me the courage to abandon all pretense at being on course. Or is this, as Simon of Taibutheh suggests, the only way one can finally discover that most mysterious principality of them all—that of the kingdom of "no-knowledge"?

A Note to the Reader

NE THING IS CERTAIN: Fra Mauro's observations on the discovery of the world have all the hallmarks of authenticity, in spite of any additions made by copyists. It may be, however, that in the act of rendering his text into English, I too have inadvertently made interpolations not a part of the original text. None of us, it seems, is exempt from the temptation of trying to improve upon the original.

This does not mean that Fra Mauro's meditations are in any way less true, for history as we know may well be no more than an elaborate fabrication on the part of scholars and historians. They are inclined to select the things they want us to believe out of the material at hand, or try to ensure that their view of events is the one we should believe rather than that of another. All I have done is echo their prediliction by exploring the remarkable subjectivity of the world in the company of Fra Mauro.

Mauro's world, as he clearly states, is an artifice. He spent a lifetime endeavoring to capture it on a piece of parchment so later generations might benefit from his labors. As noble as this attempt might have been we are nonetheless struck by how provisional his efforts appear to be today. The world he experienced is not ours. The clarity of his vision has already been eclipsed. We are left with the knowledge that were Fra Mauro alive now he would have been forced to discount most of what he had experienced.

This raises an important question. Are facts redundant, the disguise we often wear in order to conceal the emptiness we experience? Some of Mauro's informants seemed to think so. The Jew of Rhodes or that indefatigable traveler Fra Campeggio, for example, each intimates how rootlessness or decapitation may in fact camouflage a more reflective, a more perceptive view of the world. Let's not forget those Garamantes either, who were condemned to death for daring to believe in the forces of nature as harbingers of gods.

What I discovered in the library of the Mechitar Fathers on the island of San Lazzaro all those years ago turned out to be much more than the ruminations of a Renaissance cleric. Fra Mauro intimated the possibility of making a journey beyond the realm of fact, a journey to the very limits of the way we imagine our world. He alone asked me to dismiss all that I thought was certain in favor of something far more dangerous. He asked me to risk everything, my whole life perhaps, in pursuit of that painful gestation of a world fashioned by the fever and limits of the spirit.

I make no case for the veracity of Mauro's observations. They are his as much as they are mine. He and I have linked arms across time and, in a way, each of us has influenced the other. He has made me a part of his time as I have made him a part of mine. This, surely, must be the real significance of history: that it allows us the opportunity to reach back into the past, tinker with its images, and so transform it into our own.

Nonetheless, he has left me with one image I will not easily forget. As he patiently labored over his *mappa mundi* for those years, he began to recognize the power of invisible events to change the course of history. What he failed to mention, however, yet it continues to permeate his text even to this day, was the idea of an *invisible geography* affecting the way we think about place. The spirit in the world, namely the elusive power of the imagination, dominated his ruminations to the point where he, too, evidently chose to abandon all pretense at being objective. In the end, I suspect that Fra Mauro deliberately crafted himself into his map not out of a desire to trick us, but in order to alert us to the world's infinite capacity for surprise.

About the Illustrations

Fra Mauro's world map, as described in *A Map-maker's Dream,* has been lost for centuries. The illustrations that appear on the endpapers, title page, and at the beginning of each chapter are details from another work by Mauro, his only surviving *mappamundi,* preserved in the Biblioteca Nazionale Marciana in Venice. (Photographic details courtesy of Foto Tosa.)